Creative Singing

*The story of an experiment in
music and creativity in the
Primary Classroom*

KEN EVANS

London
OXFORD UNIVERSITY PRESS
NEW YORK TORONTO
1971

Oxford University Press, Ely House, London W.1

GLASGOW NEW YORK TORONTO MELBOURNE WELLINGTON
CAPE TOWN SALISBURY IBADAN NAIROBI DAR ES SALEM LUSAKA
ADDIS ABABA BOMBAY CALCUTTA MADRAS KARACHI LAHORE
DACCA KUALA LUMPUR SINGAPORE HONG KONG TOKYO

ISBN 0 19 317411 1

*Printed in Great Britain
by W & J Mackay & Co Ltd, Chatham*

Foreword

During the many years I have been associated with schools in the West Riding perhaps the feature that has given me most satisfaction has been the steady flow of research and exploratory work carried out by teachers and Advisers in every possible aspect of the educational process. To visit a primary school today is to see and hear things undreamed of 20 years ago, and this has been the outcome of the tirelessly enthusiastic work put in by countless people all aiming to improve and enrich the school years of West Riding children. It is always a pleasure to me to read an account of one or other aspect of this general and widespread activity. Ken Evans has produced in these pages an entertainingly written report on one aspect of musical work which he fostered personally when an Adviser in the county. It combines a real sense of the realities of the classroom situation with considerable distinction of thought, and I trust that it will give valuable ideas and stimulus to many teachers in primary schools. I myself have found it a pleasure to read.

SIR ALEC CLEGG MA

Chief Education Officer
County Council of the West Riding of Yorkshire

March 1971

To the liberal spirit of adventure of
West Riding teachers

Contents

Preface

I should like to acknowledge my debt to Sir Alec Clegg, Chief Education Officer, West Riding County Council, for permission to make extensive use of work from West Riding schools and, perhaps even more, for the encouragement received during my period of service with the West Riding Education Authority.

To my former colleagues of the Authority's Advisory Staff, in particular Mr. John Gavall, Senior Music Adviser, I should like to extend my thanks for long hours of stimulating discussion and planning.

It is impossible to thank all the teachers and children who have knowingly or unknowingly contributed to this book, but I cannot but mention Mrs. Mary Froggett, Miss M. Woodhead and Mr. David Street.

I am grateful to Mr. Michael Flanders for permission to quote from his 'London Transport Omnibus'.

Lastly I should like to thank my wife and children for an almost frantic forbearance during the playing of endless tape recordings, and for their help in editing the plethora of notated examples of creative work.

1 Lines of Approach

Many teachers in Infant and Junior Schools are cautious about involving themselves in music-making with their classes. This is not because they are unadventurous. The same teachers are making exciting contributions to the educational scene through experiments, involving considerable preparation and time commitment, with the 'New Mathematics', Nuffield Science, French, and many other of the current educational trends in both Infant and Junior Schools. But this adventurous approach and eagerness to experiment does not always carry over into their attitude to music in the classroom.

This book is intended both for teachers who cannot read music nor play an instrument, *and* those who possess these skills and who may find in it ideas which will extend still further their present musical activities with children. It is based upon, and follows, experiments carried out by teachers and children of Primary Schools in the West Riding of Yorkshire, and is thus an account of practice within the classroom, with quotations of music created by children of Infant and Junior age. Difficulties experienced by children and teachers are commented upon, with explanations of how these difficulties were overcome.

CREATIVE EXPRESSION BY ADULTS

Most people, at some time in the safety of their bathroom, indulge in a form of singing. Relatives or neighbours might vary in the name they give to this vocal exploration, but the fact remains that, relieved of the inhibitions caused by the external environment, and stimulated by the physical process of towelling, a great many people indulge in some form of bathroom vocalizing. If the atmosphere of the bathroom extravaganza could be taken into the Primary classrooms of the land, a musical revolution would thrust itself upon us overnight.

The football grounds of Britain, and further afield, today ring with massive vocal expression of the passions aroused by the fluctuating phases of the game. There was a time when this vocal expression consisted mainly of cheering, booing, and the permutation of a fairly limited vocabulary of abuse. Music, apart from the emotional cauldrons of South Wales Rugby, tended to be canned, or provided by a marching band. On ritual occasions like the Cup Final, a turgid, if devoted, rendering of 'Lead Kindly Light', a brighter, if tear-stained, version of 'Land of Hope and Glory', and the singing of the National Anthem were the main sum of the crowd's musical contribution.

Today the football grounds are the scene of a musical, if primitive, revolution. The social historians of the future will no doubt plough through the archives of newspapers, sound radio, and television and produce a learned treatise which will pinpoint the source and development of this phenomenon. The first evidence of the change which many people became aware of coincided with the commercial pop projection of the 'Liverpool Sound' during the height of Beatlemania:

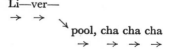

repeated endlessly, as a cry of triumph or as an exhortation that sought to stave off the ultimate disaster. Since then, this form of crowd self-expression has spread at an incredible speed. Without an organized conductor, thousands, stimulated by the excitement of the moment, club allegiance, and other artificial catalysts, chant the names of the clubs, the players, and miscellaneous comments, with a precision that would do credit to a brigade of guards.

The chanting of

had a dying fall. It is made up of two sounds, the distance between which forms the interval of what is traditionally regarded as the

call, or the falling minor third. This is the interval which Carl Orff noted to be of most common use among young children in their singing word games, and it is the first interval taught, according to the Kodaly Method, in the Hungarian schools. There, sol-fa names are used to name and identify this falling sound:—

soh
  ↘
    me.

What this book shows and suggests, drawing on activities already established in schools, is that teachers and children can combine to make use of this basic, untutored, inclination for vocal expression, and to use it in a cohesive way.

CREATIVE EXPRESSION IN YOUNG INFANTS

From the point of view of musical expression, it is unfortunate that the fascinating exploration of vocal sound that is part of the normal life of the baby in its pre-verbal stage tends to disappear when the spoken word is achieved. The mystifying gurgles, the strange meanderings high and low over a wide and picaresque vocal range, interspersed with more percussive elements, are replaced and excluded by 'ma-ma, da-da' or whatever the idiom of the locality. It is understandable that the fond parent, suffused with pride, concentrates on encouraging the acquisition of names for new objects and activities, but sad that this usually discourages the development of non-verbal vocal exploration.

Vocal musical interest consequently tends to be channelled into singing, or diverted to listening to nursery rhymes, pop songs, carols, and the like. It ceases to be creative and becomes a musical experience in which the exploration is part only of the musical performance, or the musical listening, and no longer of the *actual creation* of the music.

CREATIVE MUSIC IN SCHOOLS

When the social stage in the child's development is reached, this creative vocal element is partially recovered in the practical modifications made on traditional children's games, at home and in the playground. The use of the voice in the classroom, however, has tended to be associated in the past almost solely with the singing of songs or with sight-singing exercises. Because many otherwise gifted teachers feel that this demands ability to accompany the singing on an instrument, they may become worried when participation in music activity is suggested.

The use of tuned percussion instruments, such as chime bars, glockenspiels, and xylophones, which are part of the Carl Orff and other comparable methods, and the singing and playing on various simple instruments, which are part of BBC programmes, have helped to overcome some of this considerable worry and reluctance. The author is aware, too, through observation and commitment, of experiments with sounds recorded by children on magnetic tape, which make use of playback and editing techniques to produce exciting new sounds, as do experiments with pure electronically produced sounds and musical 'shapes' which are not based on melody and harmony. This latter type of experiment, occurring in areas as different as Yorkshire and Inner London, is an interesting part of an attempt to widen the educational area of music-making.

The account in this book of a certain type of music-making, related closely to other forms of self-expression by children and teachers in West Riding Schools, does not attempt to supersede or replace these other music activities. The potential scope of music in schools is today vast, and this book will concentrate on one area of possible activity that has been tried in practice, and has the not inconsiderable advantage of demanding no financial outlay. It demands of the teacher no more than the release and organization of an inner inclination or potential that is already being realized in its primitive form, in the playground of the school and the football grounds of the country.

Music in school is not something that should be compartmentalized. It should sometimes grow out of other activities, sometimes be the growth point from which other activities develop. It is true that there are certain aspects of music which are unique if not self-contained. But music has many parts, and music-making can often be seen in relation to, and integrated with, other educational activities, bringing with it both unity and variety in the educational process. This is why it is important that teachers should become aware of as many different opportunities as possible for children to express themselves musically.

Only a 'pedagogic mandarin'—to use a phrase coined by Sir Alec Clegg—would be sufficiently megalomaniac to suggest that any one approach is the ultimate answer to music in schools. What is suitable varies from school to school and teacher to teacher, and allows room for much experiment and diversity. That is why this book takes the form of an account of activities, and not a statement of objective truth.

In music, in all education, the real truth lies in the development of the personality of the individual child.

2 Free and Selective Vocal Exploration

Two initial approaches were used to help children to create their own music through singing. Both make use of simple word patterns—the names of children, football teams, or virtually anything of current interest that will provide a basic word rhythm. For either approach the word pattern is first spoken, with clapping, tapping, or finger clicking, to highlight the syllabic rhythm of the words.

The first approach, *free vocal exploration*, calls for a simple word pattern and the children are asked to use the words to make a short *singing* phrase. The teacher may or may not have to give a starting note. Various sung suggestions may be offered as to a suitable pitch for a particular syllable, or syllables forming a word, or the whole phrase, and the class accept or reject these through experiment. If the pitch of a single syllable is offered it is always found necessary to re-sing the notes up to that point, so that the shape of the developing phrase can be felt.

Here is an example of a first attempt by a class of 6-year-olds who offered suggestions, through singing higher or lower sounds, as to how the name should be set. No specific notation of the sounds used is given, as the children themselves were aware only of a general shape.

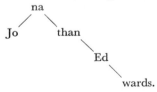

The second approach, *selective vocal exploration*, makes use of a *limited* number of specific sounds to which the children are initially restricted.

On the next page is an example of a verse made up by 5–6-year-olds, flushed with expectation of a Shrovetide tea, who were using two notes only. These two notes form the interval noted in Chapter 1 as being used by the Liverpool football crowd!

This example is a reproduction, minus the attractive colours used, of how the teacher later wrote out the song for the class. (It may be noted that the teacher was in no way a music specialist, and was herself experimenting with the children.) This song was the first of an interesting collection called 'Our Song Book', which was on display in a Music Corner and available at any time. The song, discussion about Shrove Tuesday, and paintings of the domestic pancake scene, grew up together as it were.

s   s
        m
Pancake day
s   s
        m
Pancake day
s   s
     m m
I like pancakes
s   s
     m
Any way.

These 5–6-year-olds were aware that they were using the sol-fa sounds

If the reader is unfamiliar with sol-fa notation, the striking of on chime bars, glockenspiel, or xylophone will produce a similar interval.

Classes did not adhere rigidly to either of the two approaches, but there was considerable variation between the proportion of free and selective activity with different groups of children. It is fair to say that the completely free approach tended to present more difficulties for a teacher who had no previous active experience of music and music notation, whereas the selective approach proved more acceptable and workable by such teachers.

It is true also, that with children who, through embarrassment or other factors, are somewhat reluctant to sing, it is often easier to evoke response if use is made of a limited and graduated vocabulary. At the discretion of the teacher there can, of course, be free interplay between the two approaches.

The difference between the free and selective approach presents more than a technical musical difference. On the surface, at least, it suggests a difference of educational philosophy. In the many discussions about 'creative music', as it has come to be called, a great deal of argument has developed about the respective merits of the free and selective approaches. On the one hand, it has been argued that the limiting of sound resources to be explored is bad educational practice, and unfavourable comparisons are drawn with the approach to painting where children are given a free range of material.

On the other hand, the argument is advanced that music is a language, and that, as in language, freedom of expression depends on the ability to recall past experiences, for which some form of notation is an aid.

Each approach has its own extreme. In the first extreme, the process is therapeutic rather than educational. What is expressed is no more than the most immediate sensation of the moment and there is little or no development of expression through sound. In the second extreme, an emphasis on the language of music, as opposed to expression *through* music, can lead to a sterile obsession with notation: what is written becomes more important than the sounds made.

Where the balance should be made depends on particular situations. What has been observed is that, whatever approach is used at a particular time, the emphasis on creativity has made music experience more vivid and challenging for children, and enabled music to be brought into closer synthesis with other activities.

It has been observed, too, that notation which presents a *visual picture*, whether in the form of sol-fa hand signs, the spacing of chime bars or notes on the glockenspiel, or ultimately a written notation which can be inventive or make use of the traditional stave, helps children to organize the creative use of their sound experiences.

As selective vocal exploration is a graduated approach and one more accessible to all types of teachers, musically experienced or inexperienced, greater emphasis will be given to this approach, both in the form of accounts of children's activities and in the direct suggestions made to teachers. Musically experienced teachers will at all stages see the implications for free experiment.

Although the selective approach is graduated, because the time span of the West Riding experiment did not embrace a whole generation of Primary School children, we could not see the approach at the 5-year-old stage and *with the same children* at the 10–11-year stage, even though it was used at all ages between 5 and 11. It is interesting to speculate what form the work of 10-year-olds will take who have experienced this type of creative approach from the age of 5.

QUESTION AND ANSWER

At all age levels the first approach was made through the teacher singing a question to the children as a class. The question took the form of a falling minor third: our ubiquitous interval. Here is an immediate opportunity to relate music to other activities. Use can be made of the whole range of classroom activities and questions, interesting to the particular age group, improvised from this material. This should be given not at any specific time, but fleetingly at any moment of the day. It was found that singing the question to the class generally was far better than singing to an individual child. The generality of the question did not impose the burden of response on any one individual.

Here is an example of a question asked at the beginning of a leaden-skied day, demanding no early-morning feat of imagination. At this stage, sol-fa names were not used, but they are included here for the benefit of the reader.

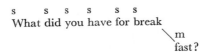

Answers

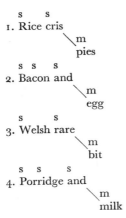

Notice the different rhythm presented by 1 and 3 as opposed to 2 and 4.

In almost all cases and with all age groups, teachers noted that the answer followed the pattern of the

question, falling a minor third at the end of the phrase.

The most obvious difficulties experienced were that some children, as the question was addressed to the class as a whole, offered no answer, and that others did not sing the reply but spoke it. If the answer was spoken, the teacher would then sing it and invite all the class to join in and repeat the answer. If no answer of any sort was forthcoming, which hardly ever happened, the teacher would set a pattern of procedure by offering an answer. The class were invited to repeat it, and this then produced a further response from the children, either sung or spoken, but which was their own.

No problems of rhythm occurred, as the rhythms of both question and answer are contained in the words. The rhythms are further heightened by being accompanied with clapping and tapping. Problems of pitch, however, were encountered. Normally children answered at the same pitch as that of the question posed by the teacher. Teachers pitched the question comfortably within their own and the children's vocal range, allowing for the octave difference of the male teacher's voice. There was no insistence on a high-pitched question and generally the questions posed were somewhere within the range of from

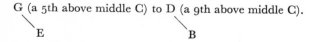

There is no need for a question to begin on a particular note, provided that the pitch is not uncomfortable for the singers.

It was occasionally found at all Primary School age levels that children responded at a pitch different from that of the teacher's question, but still falling a minor third from their starting note. This meant relatively that the answer was similar to the question. As facility was acquired the answer was given at the identical pitch to that of the question. At the other end of the ability range, musically gifted children responded freely with all sorts of florid variants on the pitch and interval of the question. This too happened rarely. It presented no problem for the musically experienced teacher when the odd flamboyant virtuoso asked for the names of the notes that had been sung. Musically inexperienced teachers in general healthily acknowledged their difficulty and sought the notation of the notes experimentally with the children, using either voices or instruments.

Very occasionally, some children either spoke the answer, or, when trying to sing, pitched differently and then could not move from the starting note, thus producing a monotone answer. These are the children who were in the past called grunters or groaners or described as 'tone deaf'. A rather amusing variant of this once emerged from the calculated wit of a forthright 6-year-old Yorkshire lad who, when asked by the teacher

What do you like for din
ner?

responded with the terse, monosyllabic, spoken

Spoods.

VOCAL SOUND

Before commenting further on the difficulties of such children, it would be well to consider the nature of vocal sound.

A great deal of harm has been done to the acceptance of singing as a normal activity through the popular use of phrases like 'He has a marvellous voice', or 'She was born with a voice'. These expressions suggest that, unless you have been given some extraordinary gift, you are barred for life from really enjoying the act of singing.

Paradoxically, this attitude is often strongest in areas with great choral traditions and where highly specialized choirs have developed, and, ironically, is now disappearing among young people as the result of commercial exploitation of the pop music scene. It is, however, an attitude which prevails among many teachers who are timorous of taking their private vocalizing into the classroom.

If the ability to sing is disassociated from the belief that it is some mysterious gift bestowed on the few, and instead understood as a process of mental and physical co-ordination that develops through experience, though at different rates of speed, the way to progressive vocal expression will have been opened to teachers and children. Put simply, what happens in singing is that sound is conceived mentally, the vocal chords respond to this mental demand and adjust themselves so that, when vibrated by the air expelled from the lungs, the vibration produces the pitch demanded by the brain. As when learning to walk, individuals do not develop the mental/physical co-ordination at the same pace. But a slow infant walker is not discouraged from walking.

Obviously, great natural endowment will allow some infant walkers to develop into top-class athletes and some infant singers into famous performers. But as almost all can at some level enjoy a form of physical activity that expresses itself in games or outdoor pursuits, so almost all can enjoy the form of physical activity that expresses itself in singing.

In classrooms where the sung 'Question and Answer' became, at odd moments, a normal part of the school day, often providing a source of light relief as tired minds faltered, *all* children eventually developed the ability to pitch accurately. Not all produced the beautiful vocal sound of the gifted few, but not all of them, either, would be capable of the feats of the few gifted athletes. This was not important for the vast majority of the children. What the children, and, indeed, many of the teachers were being given for the first time was a new and unembarrassed source of self-expression and self-discipline.

NOTATING THE PITCH OF 'QUESTION AND ANSWER'

The latest research suggests very strongly that visual images, suggesting the comparative relationship between notes of different pitch, help children to develop pitch discrimination. Consequently, right from the beginning, our teachers accompanied the questions sung to the children not only with tapping, but with hand patterns in the air which suggested the falling third interval at the end of each question. Some used arbitrary signs of high and low, but all, eventually even with 5-year-olds, made use of the sol-fa hand signs* for

This occurred *before* the actual sol-fa names were introduced.

The children, without any encouragement, often made use of the same hand signs in their answer. Certainly, when an individual answer had been given, the teacher and class made use of this visual aid to pitch discrimination in repeat-

* See table of hand signs, p. 95.

ing the reply. The answer, therefore, could be accompanied by tapping and clicking, or hand signs, or both.*

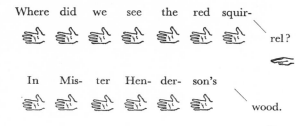

Where did we see the red squirrel?

In Mis- ter Hen- der- son's
wood.

Next came the explanation that as in language we have names for particular objects and activities, so in music we have names for particular sounds. The teacher then made use of the question and answer of the moment. These were repeated, this time *without words*, but using instead the sol-fa names to the same rhythms, accompanied as before by hand signs.

The red squirrel question would then emerge as:

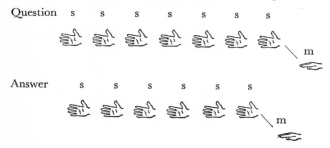

Question s s s s s s s
m

Answer s s s s s s
m

In this way music notation, in elementary form, was presented not as something abstract and academic, but as a means of recording what had been created, however simply, by the children. It was found that this visual recording of the

* See table of hand signs, p. 95.

music created stimulated the children, and helped them to build up a conscious vocabulary of sound.

VERSE SETTING

When the daily singing of Question and Answer, accompanied by tapping and hand signs, had been established as a normal activity—and this sometimes happened within a very few days—the teacher proceeded to encourage children to extend the use of words and to set them to a two-note tune using

The 'Pancake Day' song is a typical example of words and music made up by Infants. Here is another two-note Infant song conditioned by British weather, and with a reference to Timbuctoo that must have had its origin in domestic frustration.

```
s     s    s s
              m  m
Wind was very windy
s  s     s
          m m
It blew me away
s  s    s   s
             m   m  m
It blew me to Timbuctoo
s   s  s
        m    m
I'll be back someday.
```

This song was made up through discussion and experiment between the children and teacher.

Junior age children often responded with such facility to the

Question and Answer that, within a few days, the same approach was used with

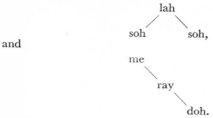

and

These Questions and Answers formed a slightly enlarged vocabulary.

Here is a first attempt to make up verse and music by a class of 7-year-olds, who added some weird and appropriate sound effects. They appear to have either scorned the thought of rhyme or found it unsuitable or unattainable.

```
s  s          s  s
     m             m
Astronauts   Astronauts

s     s    l        s
Whizzing through space

s  s          s  s
     m             m
Astronauts   Astronauts

s     s
          m  r   d
Landing on the moon.
```

Note the reliance on soh as a starting point at this stage.

The approach was the same for Infant and Junior children. For simplicity of illustration we will look at the approach of an Infant class, which in a very short time had mastered the soh

```
        \
          me
```

type of Question and Answer. The words had already been made up and written down on a chalkboard. The teacher suggested procedure.

We'll begin by singing soh.

This was established and sung together with hand sign. The teacher then asked:

What shall we have next, soh or

me?

   To start with, it was a piecemeal form of creation. But gradually children offered more than just one note and began to think in fragments of phrases, or even whole phrases. From the start it was found absolutely essential to sing the phrase again from the beginning after each note was added, before anything more was added to it. This developed a sense of musical shape in the children, and helped them to appreciate sounds not as separate entities but in the context of the phrase.

   Two difficulties were experienced. 1. As in the Question and Answer approach, sometimes the note offered by a child would be spoken, not sung. 2. Sometimes the child would sing the *pitch* of the note soh, but use the *word* 'me', or vice versa.

   The first difficulty was met by the teacher singing, on an indeterminate vowel sound, 'ooh', the pitch of both soh and me, and asking: 'Which sound did you want?' Then the teacher sang the correct name to the sound chosen and all were invited to repeat the phrase up to that point.

   The second difficulty was met in a similar way. Using a vowel sound which was not part of the sol-fa vocabulary, the teacher repeated the pitch of the misnamed sound given by the pupil and asked: 'Is this the sound you wanted?' If the answer was yes, the teacher explained what was the correct name for that sound, and all sang it together. If the answer was no, the teacher sang the pitch of the other optional note or notes on an indeterminate vowel sound, the sound finally chosen was then named and again all resung the phrase up to that point.

This might sound a slow and rather tedious process. The proportion of the children's responses which presented such difficulties was, however, small and became progressively smaller as facility was acquired. Indeed, the momentum built up between children and teacher, as the song was resung from the beginning and seen to grow and grow, made for increasing excitement not tedium.

When the songs were complete, other forms of activity added to the interest aroused: paintings, models depicting the scene, and, in the case of a narrative song, creative play which grew out of the narrative at Junior level, or a more organized dramatization of the story. The following example offered such scope. It was made up by a class of 6-year-olds who had been using this type of creative approach for some twelve months. They had been encouraged to experiment with contrasting effects obtained by giving certain lines or verses to solo voice, duo, or trio, or to the whole class.

It is interesting to note which words have obviously grown from the dramatic imagination of the children and which have been influenced by familiar hymns.

By the time this song was made up the children had become familiar with

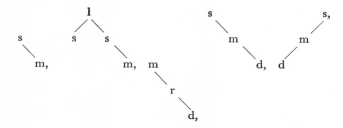

and had themselves decided to use the note (fah) between soh and me, whose name they requested. Each verse was sung to the tune set to the first verse. The verses were, of course, made up orally.

He took the name Jesus

```
          l
s            s
                m   m
                 d
```
Where are you going to

```
    l
s       s
            m
              d
```
Joseph and Mary?

```
          l
       s     s
m               m   m
                 d
```
We're going to Bethlehem

```
f
    m
      r
        d
```
Taxes to pay.

Inns are so crowded there
Joseph and Mary
There's only a stable
In which you can stay.

The cows and the horses
Will keep out the cold winds
And God will take care of us
All through the night.

A baby was born to
Joseph and Mary
He took the name Jesus
And he is our Lord.

We are the shepherds
We've come from the hillside
The Angels have told us
A baby is born.

Frankincense gold and myrrh
We bring to Jesus
We followed a shining star
To Bethlehem

All little children
Are thinking of Jesus
The Lord of Creation
Our Saviour and King.

Needless to say a pseudo-Handelian rallentando accompanied the last line.

Apart from the distribution of lines, some of which was implicit in the words, it was interesting that some of the children were able to accompany the tune with a repetitive lulling,

which thus formed an ostinato to some verses. This was the beginning of part singing.

CLASS, GROUP, AND INDIVIDUAL WORK

In Primary education today the class has become less and less the activity unit. In most activities, because of the recognition that children develop in different ways and at different speeds, the activity unit has become that of a small group, or the individual child. The initial class approach to this type of creative music-making therefore needs some explanation.

When children come to school, almost all, apart from the severely handicapped, can talk. They are aware of names

given to certain objects and activities, *not just of an environment in which the use of words occurs.* They have all used these
words, first imitatively, and then manipulating them to express themselves in situations not previously experienced.
They have in fact used words creatively to express themselves.
Since pre-verbal vocal exploration is rejected in favour of
word exploration, children do not normally enter school able
to manipulate sounds so well as they can words. Generally,
through the mass media and from other sources, they are
aware of an environment in which sounds occur, but they
have not made use of sounds to express themselves in a
creative musical way.

The initial class approach to creative singing attempts to
provide not just an environment in which the use of sounds
occurs. It aims at helping children to acquire, in a much
shortened time, the sort of conscious awareness of sounds and
the ability to manipulate them that parents, in the pre-
school stage, have helped children to acquire with words.
For reasons of time and numbers, the type of slow and inti-
mate acquisition of conscious word vocabulary which occurs
under constant parental guidance in the home is not possible in the classroom. Because of this the awareness and use of
sounds is first stimulated through the class unit approach.

But there is another reason for this inclination to begin
with a group so large as the class. The nature of music-
making is such that, over and above the individual musical
self-expression, creative or interpretive, a particular emotional experience attaches itself to singing as a member of a
large group. Some other activities may also be communal in
character, but the emotional experience derived from communal music-making is something that is peculiar and
unique to music. The use of the class as the unit for music-
making has, therefore, a particular social and emotional
significance.

Once the creative approach has developed, however, and

if the physical accommodation allows, children can also be encouraged to work in smaller groups or as individuals. This will permit a pattern of development where flexibility of grouping can be used to meet the varying needs of the children.

The role of the teacher, however, is vital, both as the stimulus to the development and expression of sound vocabulary, and as the adviser to the working groups. The ways in which Yorkshire teachers stimulated the gradual development of resources for creative expression will be discussed in the following chapters.

3 Teacher and Children

As in any area of activity that is both vital and vitalizing, winds of controversy are blowing through education. Ranging from disciples of Piaget to the subscribers to the 'Black Papers', education opinion is in a state of considerable agitation. Among issues central to the debate is that of the role of the teacher in relation to the child. Discovery, experiment, analysis, discipline: these are terms in continual use by apologists. This book does not attempt to align itself with any particular faction. It is an empirical record, and any implications and positive suggestions can be interpreted and applied according to the ethos of the reader.

What has been observed is that creative vocal expression often needs to be stimulated with examples set by the teacher, and that both large and small groups and individual experiment can benefit from the advice of the teacher.

In both free and selective vocal exploration, immediate contact between children and teacher is vital. As in language development, the reaction of the child depends very much on face-to-face communication, and the interaction of the personalities of teacher and pupil. This is, of course, something not confined to music but common to many classroom situations.

The significance of this relationship for free vocal exploration, which does not make use of a graduated vocabulary of sound but in which children immediately experiment with all available vocal sounds, will be discussed later. Its significance for selective vocal exploration is also paramount. It is an integral part of the way in which a conscious acquisition of resources for creative expression develops. Besides this personal interaction, it was found, as previously mentioned, that selective activity benefited from, and lent itself to, the use of symbols, whether verbal or of sign form. These help to record and recall previous creative work, and form an immediate language of communication. Reference has been made in Chapter 2 to the use of hand signs as symbols. These were very much a part of the face-to-face communication between children and teacher, and amongst children themselves and perhaps merit a little more comment.

HAND SIGNS

The history of sol-fa hand signs need not concern us, but nearly all teachers making creative use of sol-fa found hand signs invaluable. The hand signs present the children with not only a visual distinction between higher and lower notes, but also exact symbols to distinguish the relationship between the pitch of one note and another. From the outset the signs were associated with phrases made up by the children. The first approach was of the type quoted in Chapter 2, where the question and answer

> Where did we see the red squirrel?
> In Mr. Henderson's wood,

made use both in question and answer of a repeated soh, with a fall to me on the last syllable of the line. Minus the words, the word rhythms were sung to 'soh', 'me', with the hand signs indicating visually the relative pitch of the sounds.

One of the important points to be noted about the symbolizing and naming of the relationships between sounds is that this *followed* the use of these sounds by the children. Unlike some approaches to music in the classroom, the children were not first presented with symbols, told what sounds they represented, and then invited to make use of them. The

signs and names were used by the children to record the
sounds made up by them and to assist their further communication.

An illustration of this can be seen in the carol quoted at
the end of the last chapter. The existing vocabulary of
s l s m r d was insufficient for the children, who wished to use
the sounds f m r d for the last line of the verses. They did not
know the name nor sign for fah, and asked the teacher for
help. The ability to record this sound and to use its hand
sign then became an established extension of their conscious
vocabulary of sounds.

This would mean that the first verse of the carol 'He took
the name Jesus', would have had the hand signs added to the
singing of the words or the sol-fa syllables.*

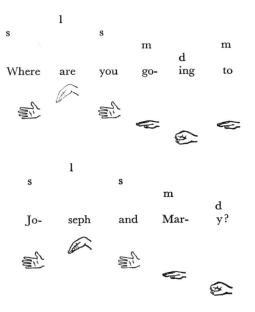

```
          l
   s            s
                   m          m
                      d
   Where  are  you  go-  ing  to
```

```
          l
   s            s
                   m
                      d
   Jo-  seph  and  Mar-  y?
```

* See table of hand signs, p. 95.

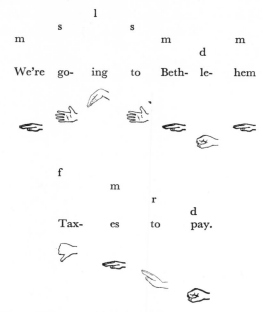

           l
     s   s
m   m   m
                  d

We're go- ing to Beth- le- hem

    f
         m
             r
                d

Tax-   es   to pay.

A Junior schoolteacher who was enthusiastically involved in this type of work told a story of being stopped, in the main street of a small town, by a bewildered local councillor. He had observed on repeated summer evenings the activities of a number of children from the school. Seated on a low wall outside the local Clinic, the children had been having great fun making up tunes to their own words. This the worthy councillor had stopped to observe and enjoy, but when he asked them how they managed to make up their tunes they had replied, as he put it, with 'Funny signs in the air'. What was really interesting was how the enthusiasm generated in the classroom had carried over into after-school play.

The official visit of an eminent political figure to the area had produced a satirical song, which could hardly have been openly created within the school walls without uncomfortable repercussions. A teacher aware of the activities of the school 'underground' brought to unofficial light a *written* manuscript of the song. Having made up the song the children had felt the need to record the words and music on paper.

One of the points is that if the teacher makes an uninhibited approach to vocal creativity the response of the *generality*, not only the 'musically gifted' of the children, is enthusiastic and energetic. A second point is that many children reject the formal approach to sight-reading, where notation on the stave or of sol-fa or their dual use is presented directly to them. But these same children, through the desire to record the tunes made up by themselves, can actually come to demand acquaintance with forms of notation.

More will be said of this later. At this stage it is sufficient to emphasize the fun that the children obtained from song-making with sol-fa and hand signs. This emphasis is necessary as the childhood acquaintance of many teachers with sol-fa and hand signs was found to have been one of rigid modulator manipulation, where a jabbing pointer had dictated the day and also acted as a convenient disciplinary weapon. This ogre picture was still found to condition the response of some teachers to the idea of using hand signs. It was not until they saw the way children enjoyed making use of them creatively that they were convinced that some old childhood nightmare was not to be visited on their children.

The hand signs* used for l s m r d were in descending order

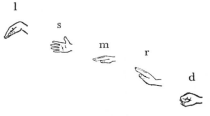

* See table of hand signs, p. 95.

The sign used for top doh was the same as that for doh, but held at a higher elevation.

Some explanation should be offered for the omission of te and fah, producing as it does a five-note, or pentatonic, scale. Both the Carl Orff Method and the Choral Method of Zoltán Kodály initially make considerable use of a five-note scale. More than one reason is advanced for this. Certainly the pattern of graduated intervals noted in Chapter 2 is often found in children's traditional song games. Is it because they are easily singable or is there some deeper genetic reason?

One of the reasons advanced by Kodály for the use of this scale is that there are no half-tones in it of the kind that occur between

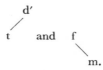

According to Kodály it is these semitones that are most difficult to sing in tune.

Whatever the reasons advanced, it was found in the classroom that, when using the voice creatively, the children's confidence generally increased more rapidly when the five-note scale was used. Once this confidence was established the children themselves demanded the extension of the scale. They wanted to use the whole range of the major scale d r m f s l t d' and some adventurous minds probed still further afield in free exploration. This was not surprising for, whereas Hungarian folk music makes great use of the pentatonic scale, its use in folk music of other lands varies enormously.

When te and fah had been used by the children, they were introduced to the sign for te 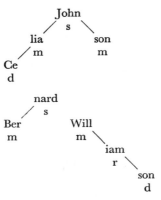 and for fah they were offered the choice between the traditional British and the Hungarian . A playground fight between two 8-year-olds was caused by disagreement as to the correct sign for fah. Their class had not yet 'officially' used the fah sign, but demonstrations of the thumb sign had been given by children from another class. This had outraged one of the boys, whose father, a stalwart of the local male voice choir, had illustrated the melancholy drooping finger fah. Such controversy does music engender.

SOCIAL SINGING GAMES

Some classes from Infant to Junior age level took such pleasure in singing with hand signs that, in addition to using them in the creative way mentioned, they devised various forms of play. These helped in establishing firmly an awareness of intervals and refined the children's aural perception. In some classes children made up a sol-fa phrase to the syllabic rhythm of their names.

```
              John
            /   s   \
        lia         son
      /   m           m
    Ce
    d

          nard
        /   s        Will
    Ber             m   \
    m                     iam
                          r   \
                              son
                              d
```

On their various writing books the pitch of the notes of these tunes would be written under their names.

At odd moments of the day the normal social intercourse of the classroom would be enlivened by interjections of the following sort. (The angular lines represent the approximate rise and fall of the sung sounds.)

Pupil: May I help ⌒⌄ with his model?

Teacher: Where is ⌄⌒⌄ ?

Pupil: I'm here.

Teacher: May ⌄⌒ help you with your model?

The sung names were either expressed through sol-fa or sung on an indeterminate vowel sound. At other moments the names would not be sung, but be signified silently with hand signs. Sometimes the singing and hand signs would accompany each other.

This all seemed at first acquaintance more than a little crazy, an extract from a Spike Milligan fantasy, but the children were seen to enjoy it all immensely. The snippets of conversation on any topic of current interest, with hand signs or sol-fa names interjected, made the use of the singing voice a normal, if somewhat unconventional classroom activity, and not something appealing only to the musically gifted.

Social singing of this sort, apart from establishing music as a normal part of the school day, meant that all members of the class became familiar in an informal way with the particular melodic fragments that made up the sung names of other members of the class. These phrases were established mentally, not by dint of boring repetition but by their use in what were often highly amusing group situations.

EXTENDING THE VOCABULARY

In Chapter 2 the procedure of class song construction was described in detail. It was pointed out that to start with it was a piecemeal form of creation, a note by note process, but that gradually children began to think in fragments of phrases or whole phrases. The addition of a new interval to the sound vocabulary, coming either through experiment by the children or its introduction by the teacher, was consolidated using the new sounds in Question and Answer, and phrases using the names of football teams, television personalities and programmes, and the like.

To illustrate this. Let us imagine that the children have included the sound of fah for the first time in their song-making, as, for instance, in the carol previously quoted. This is extending themselves beyond their 'named vocabulary'. It is a sound they wanted to use and this process is an example of free exploration following on selective exploration. (Often it was found that the confidence established through the selective exploration later encouraged a more adventurous free exploration, a basis of creative procedure having been established through the graduated approach.)

This conscious awareness of the note now named 'fah' would be consolidated through use in Question and Answer using hand signs. The questions and answers could come from both teachers and children.

```
      s     s    s    s     s     s
Q. What   did  you   do    on    Sa-
                                     \
                                       f
                                      tur-
                                          \
                                            m
                                          day?
```

Hand signs accompany all the following Questions and Answers.

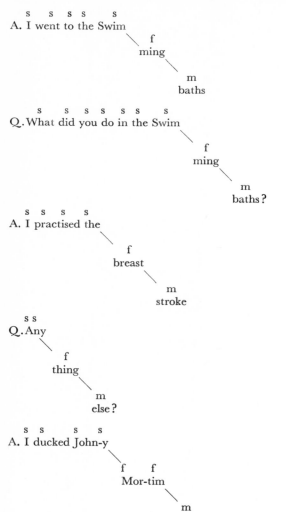

```
      s   s   s  s      s
A. I went to the Swim
                      \   f
                       ming
                            \
                             m
                            baths

      s    s   s  s   s  s   s
Q. What did you do in the Swim
                             \   f
                              ming
                                  \
                                   m
                                  baths?

     s  s   s   s
A. I practised the
                  \
                   f
                  breast
                        \
                         m
                        stroke

   s s
Q. Any
      \
       f
      thing
           \
            m
           else?

   s  s    s   s
A. I ducked John-y
                  \
                   f   f
                  Mor-tim
                         \
                          m
                         ore
```

Names of football teams, television personalities and programmes:

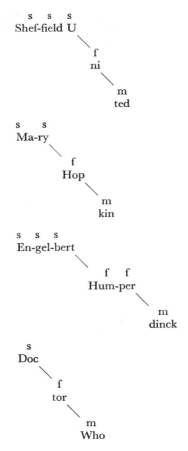

WORDS AND MUSIC

In Question and Answer, words and music were created
simultaneously. When a couplet was set to sol-fa sounds,

however, the usual procedure was for the words to be made up separately and then to be set to music although in some cases the two grew up together. One organizational point is that in some schools a music specialist is responsible for music. If so, it is very often not possible in the limited time with any class other than his own for the music specialist to discuss the making up of the words to be set. This creates the need for considerable liaison with his colleagues.

In such schools it proved best for all class teachers to be involved in the creative work, usually but not invariably making use of the selective approach, with the music specialist acting as an internal music adviser. The thought that only a music specialist can attempt this kind of work is one to be immediately rejected. At certain stages some specialist advice may be desirable, if for instance the children want help in writing their work on the stave and the class teacher is not familiar with staff notation. The notation is, however, always secondary to the sound, and even if the help desired is not available, the exploration of sounds and their expressive relation to words is of sufficient value in itself to warrant an attempt by any teacher with any class.

While most of the younger children were happy for quite a time with making up simple couplets to be set as song, the older pupils quickly demanded something of greater length and substance. It was interesting to note, too, the frequent interaction between the use of words and of sounds. At one school two 9-year-old boys, previously slow readers and reluctant in their use of language, found that the making of tunes was something they could do with increasing facility. As they wished to make up their own words to set to music their facility with language developed. The converse also occurred, where readiness to experiment with sound received a fillip from the realization that this could be related to skill in the use of language.

Where time was short, it was found helpful to make use of

written verse from anthologies in addition to words created
by the children. Further, limericks were found useful in
giving the older children, as soon as possible, a feeling that
they were setting a whole verse as opposed to individual
couplets. The only danger was that it did sometimes present
a teacher with censorship problems!

Here are two settings of the same limerick, the first by
10-year-olds who had been introduced to this approach
some three weeks previously, the second by a similar year
group who had been working this way for some five weeks.
The settings were made up on a class basis using the chalkboard. Various contributions were made, and the children
finally decided which sounds to accept after trying various
alternatives. By the time this degree of facility had been
achieved some of the children would be developing work in
groups as well as in a class unit.

1.   s   s l   s m m   r m m
      There was an old Lady whose folly
2.   d   m m s l   s   m s s

1. s   s l s m m r m m
   Induced her to sit in a holly:
2. d   m m s l s m s s

1. s   d′ s m   s
   Whereupon by a thorn
2. s   m s s   s

1. s   d′ s m   s
   Her dress being torn
2. s   m s s   s

1. s   s   l s m   m r m m
   She quickly became melancholy.
2. d   m   m s l   s m s s

The reason for the use of this type of verse was the obvious one that lines 1, 2, and 5, and lines 3 and 4 have identical rhythms. The children thus had to set to music only two lines, the first and the third, and by appropriate repetition could then sing the complete stanza to their own music.

In this way limericks, and other verse which lent itself to somewhat similar type of setting, helped to meet the early demands for verse of more than couplet length. It further created an awareness of literary and musical form reflected in the work of children in which words and music were *both* their own.

PRACTICAL CONSIDERATIONS

Whether the children were working in groups or as a class, it was found essential to reach some agreement about the rhythm of the words. Having decided on the sounds to be set to the syllables and having written the sol-fa notes down above or below the words, the children were able to sing the *sol-fa notes* to this rhythm. In the early stages only a substantial minority of children, however, were able to sing the *words* to the written pitch at a first attempt. Laboured repetition was, however, avoided. The song became part of the children's repertoire and, as facility increased, the ability to take in at a glance the words and sol-fa names, and to sing the words at the agreed pitch, progressed rapidly.

As in all relationships between teacher and children, one of the teacher's roles was to recognize a desire by individuals or groups, or even the class as a whole, to take the exploration a stage further. In most cases the signs were explicit demands by the children for the use of new sound materials, and enquiries about different techniques, of the use of round, and accompaniment. These demands could range from children involved in free exploration asking for advice on notation, to others wishing to extend their graduated vocabulary or develop new ways of using it creatively.

New advances in sound sequences were almost invariably consolidated through their use in Question and Answer and word jingles. This helped to ensure that the use of new sounds was not just something particular to a single instance but something that could be recalled for use on any occasion.

Apart from the desire to use *instrumental* sound with voices, which will be referred to later, one of the early demands was for experiments with two or more sounds sung at the same time. In other words, for some harmony or very basic part-singing. The next chapter describes some of the ways that this developed.

4 Simultaneous Sounds

One of the earliest experiments with a combination of simultaneous sounds was that of the carol quoted in Chapter 2. The accompanying of the melody by the lulling s

                                       \
                                         m

could hardly be called producing a second part or, apart from the last line, as suggesting harmony. But the suggestion is there, if only accidentally, and if the reader can inveigle some reluctant hero into singing the falling s—m interval as an accompaniment to the melody sung slowly, then the harmonic effect of the last line will be appreciated.

```
        Where are you go-ing to
          s    l   s   m  d  m
          s———————   m————
        Jo-seph and Ma-ry?
         s  l    s   m  d
         s———————   m————
        We're going to Beth-le-hem
          m  s  l  s   m  d  m
         ——  s———    m————
        Tax-es to pay.
          f  m r    d
         s————    m
```

Here is another example of the simultaneous use of more than one vocal sound by 6-year-olds. It comes from a story made up by one child. The other children, after discussion with the teacher, felt that the story lent itself to song setting and a co-operative effort resulted. The musical story with a woodland setting was called *Sarah and the Witch*. In the example, the knowledgeable trees represented by one group of children are, with great concern, warning Sarah to take care. The grasses, represented by a second group in the role of a Greek chorus, comment sadly: 'Sarah wouldn't listen.'

Group 1 sings first and then Group 2, with earnest faces expressing the imminence of impending doom, add *their* vocal line:

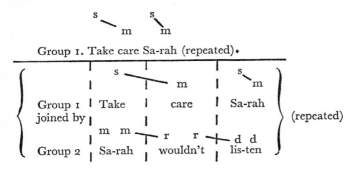

Here we have the combined sounds s m, m r, s d, m d, created by the use of a s-m ostinato joined by the rhythmic melodic phrase of m m r r d d. The harmonic effects here again are incidental but possibly more positive than in the carol. Later, ostinato was much used by children of Junior school age, in its own right, as a means of embellishing the simple melodies they had created.

THE USE OF ROUNDS

Incidental harmony also arose when Junior children who had been singing traditional rounds desired to make rounds of their own.

Here is a setting of *Jabberwocky* by first-year Juniors. When tried out as a round, interesting combinations of sounds resulted. In addition to the chance combination of notes forming the intervals of a third and a fifth, the intervals of a fourth, second, and seventh occurred. The round was sung by two groups. When the first group had sung 'Jabberwock Jabberwock,' the second group entered with the same words, as the first group proceeded to 'great big ugly beast'. This song stimulated considerable expression with paint.

```
m  m  m      s  s   s       d  d   r r   m
Jabberwock, Jabberwock, great big ugly beast

s   s  d'    d'  s    s    m
Eyes of flame and teeth like spears

r    r   r    r   m  m  m
Massive spikes and claws of steel

s     s      m m  d  d  d
Please don't make a feast of me
```

As with ostinato, the round was later much used to embellish simple song settings.

CONSECUTIVE CHORD NOTES

Among other factors, such experiences of 'incidental harmony' led Junior children to wish to use harmony positively in their song making. Although they were familiar with relatively discordant sounds from singing their own songs as rounds, the children's immediate inclination was to sing block harmonies of the traditional kind. An exception was a minority accustomed to a mainly free melodic approach who wished to experiment with a free harmonic combination of all possible vocal sounds.

In the majority of cases, the creative experiments with combined vocal sounds, whether free or traditional, were not at first successful. It had, however, become obvious from the melodic patterns created by children using the whole scale, d r m f s l t d', that a strong subsconcious awareness of traditional chords existed. This was observed even at Infant level and had presumably been conditioned by various musical factors, commercial and otherwise. But though the inclination was strong, it could not at first be creatively translated into vocal harmony.

As a help towards developing harmonic awareness, the children of the majority, whose attraction to traditional harmonies was strong, were encouraged to use the melodic form of these chords in their song settings. Although experiments with combined vocal sounds continued on a 'selective' and 'free' basis, to a degree, what immediately follows is an outline of the melodic expression of the traditional chord sequences to which children were attracted. The simplest of these were the basic chords built on rising intervals of the third, d-m-s, f-l-d', s-t-r', used by Infant and Junior children.

These notes would be sung consecutively, with almost all the children wishing to end on top doh.

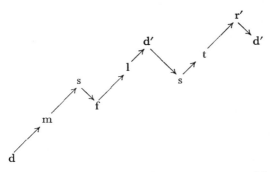

Experiments with various rhythmic patterns would occur. Here is an example of the same series sung by 6-year-olds to a slow waltz rhythm.

d	m	s	f	l	d′	s	t	r′	d′	–	–
1	2	3	1	2	3	1	2	3	1	2	3

The children fitted words to the series. Some of the words took the form of Question and Answer, modified to allow more than one syllable to each note of each chord.

Where are you go-ing to when you go home?
  d m s f l d′ s t r′ d′

I'm go-ing to the shop and I'm buy-ing some gum.
  d d d m s f   l d′   s t r′   d′.

As the children would have had considerable experience of using sol-fa names of the whole of the major scale before beginning to sing these note patterns, there was no hostility when they were introduced in this way. Nevertheless, some teachers preferred to introduce these pitch patterns first through word jingles and then invited the children to give the sol-fa names of the notes used. Decisions of this sort depended on children's age and rate of aural development, and in most instances a combination of the two approaches was used.

Making use of this series, with some melodic adaptations, a class of 6-year-olds produced a hymn with words following a rather conventional hymn idiom.

  d m s f l d′
Thank you for being there

  s t   r′ d′
All through the night

  d m s f l d′
Thank you for being there

  s t   r′ d′
All through the day

r′   t t   d′ s s
Thank you for ma-king us

r′   t t   d′ s   s
Thank you for lov-ing us

d   m s f   l d′
Thank you for kee-ping us

s   t r′ d′
Hap-py and gay

Junior school children were eager to use the selective chord notes in the chanting of names of football teams and those of popular figures of the entertainment world.

Leeds U-ni-ted Ever-ton
  d m s s   f l   d′

Tot-ten-ham Hot-spur too.
  s s   t   r′ r′ d′

Her-man and the Her-mits
  d   d   m m   s   s

Dus-ty Spring-field
  f   l   d′ d′

En-gel-bert Hum-per-dinck
 s   s   t   r′   r′   d′

The discussion and selection of words, and the process of deciding what syllables to set using chord notes, were often hilarious and groups competed in searching for incisive and often bizarre rhythms. It was generally found that children would extend this approach without any prompting and their experiments with the selective chord notes used became more adventurous.

Where the word rhythms were created first, children later sang the sol-fa sounds with or without hand signs to the word rhythms already used. This would always be accompanied by some form of non-pitch rhythm: clapping, tapping, the use of bongos and other suitable instruments. After experience of this rhythmic singing, using chord notes associated with word rhythms, some children would experiment with abstract rhythms not associated with words. These abstract rhythms might be explored through clapping, drumming, and then having the sol-fa chord notes added. This practice was rare.

By the time the desire for this experiment had come the children would feel the rhythm and pitch as a *joint* experience. Possible rhythm phrases would be explored through the rhythmic singing of the chord notes, perhaps accompanied by hand drums. Here we had an interesting combination of the free and selective approach. The approach to the rhythm was free, that to the pitch selective, in the sense that choice of notes was predetermined by the chord formations. It is difficult to put down on paper examples of the rhythms used without having recourse to complex notation. Here, however, is a very simple example of one of the first attempts by 8-year-olds to use sol-fa chord notes without first establishing word patterns.

d   d   m   s   m
quick slow quick slow slow

f   f   l   d'   l
quick slow quick slow slow

s   s   t   r'   t
quick slow quick slow slow

d'   d'   s   s   m   d
quick quick quick quick slow slow

It might be thought that the next step the children might have taken would have been experiment with free rhythm, and pitch derived from chords made up of *any* cluster of notes, or a turning away from harmonic resources and a return to free melodic experiment.

This did not happen except in very few isolated instances. The question and inquiry that might have led to the type of experiment with free harmonies was not posed until the children had developed the ability to sing the chord notes harmonically, with the simultaneous combination of sounds.

The rhythmic experiment with the chord notes of the basic traditional chords developed a confidence in the children that led them to using the chordal patterns for more extended word settings. This activity ran parallel with the free rhythmic singing of sol-fa chord notes.

Here is a typical example of a group setting of words made

up by an individual 8-year-old. The chord formation is
almost entirely predictable, but within the limits they set
themselves the decisions were arrived at 'democratically'.
As so often happened, Art work in paint, various forms of
collage, accompanied the creative work with words and
music, ranging from representation of lugubrious faces con-
templating the weather to more abstract and surrealist
impressions of 'Rain'.

In discussion the children unanimously agreed on the
chord d-m-s as a starting point. Considerable argument
about where changes of chord notes might occur led to vocal
experiment. The sounds to be used for lines 2 and 3 were
particularly controversial, with some lively exchange of
views, too, about the notes to be used for the last line. Some
favoured a change somewhere in the middle of the last line,
others wanted different chord notes. After continually trying
out various possibilities this was the final conclusion arrived
at.

(Using notes of chord d-m-s for lines 1 and 2)
Pit pat pit pat go the drops of rain
 d m s m s   s   s   s m

Drip drop drip drop there they go a-gain
  s   m   s   m   d d   d d s

(Using notes of chord f-l-d' for line 3)
Some are big and some are small
  f   f   f   l   d'   d'   l

(Using notes of chord d-m-s for line 4)
  I don't like the rain at all
  s s   m m s   s   s

(Using notes of chord s-t-r' for line 5)
But sometimes I sit and think
  s t   t   t r' r'   r'

(Using notes of chord d-m-s for the last line)
What they'd be like if they were pink
  d'   d'   d' d' d' d   d   d

CHORD NOTES USED HARMONICALLY

The point at which children thought of using harmonically the chord notes to which they were attracted, varied enormously. For some it was an early step. Others did not conceive of such a use until they heard other children experimenting with harmony or the teacher suggested it.

It was rare that Junior children, or for that matter the younger Secondary School children, could sing a complete chord at the first attempt. That is, few children, when they divided into three groups, with group 1 singing doh, group 2 me, and group 3 soh, were able to sing these notes simultaneously.

In spite of this, all the children soon found that they could experiment with harmony, by one group singing and sustaining the root note and other groups adding the other notes one by one. This built-up harmony was almost always a necessary transition between singing detached notes of a chord melodically, and singing a chord in which all the notes began simultaneously. As with other new elements in their sound vocabulary, use was made of Question and Answer and lively word rhythms.

Here is an example of Question and Answer sung rapidly and built upwards from doh begun by Group 1. Each group, apart from the first, enters as the preceding group sustains the 'day' in 'Saturday'. (Read the example from the bottom upwards).

Group 3 Where are you go-ing on Sa-tur-day? (sustained)
           s← s s s s s s   s

Group 2 Where are you go-ing on Sa-tur-day? (sustained)
           m← m m m m m m m m

Group 1 Where are you going on Sa-tur-day? (sustained)
begins   d   d   d d d d d d   d

The answering groups build up the chord in the same way.

Group 6 That's my sec-ret! (sustained)
       s   s   s   s

Group 5 That's my secret! (sustained)
       m   m   m m

Group 4 That's my sec-ret! (sustained)
begins   d   d   d   d

Name rhythms were used in a similar way.

     Group 3   Shef-field U-ni-ted
               s   s   s s

     Group 2   Shef-field U-ni-ted
               m   m   m m m

     Group 1   Shef-field U-ni-ted
     begins   d   d   d d

When Group 3, in the above example, had joined in and sung the words a few times, the last syllable of U-ni-ted was finally sustained by all groups.

The sounding of the composite notes of the chord greatly excited children. The excitement of some 9-year-old children in a school in a socially deprived area stays in the memory as a wonderful example of animated response from children too often conditioned out of school to a deadening lethargy. And this is to understate rather than overstate the impact of vocal harmony and its later creative use on these children.

Having established the singing of the d-m-s chord through a varied melodic and rhythmic build-up that *became* harmony through sustaining each chord note at the end of a line, the chords of f-l-d' and s-t-r' were also built up in the same way. No difficulties were experienced, as considerable melodic experiment with d-m-s, f-l-d', s-t-r', in the form of Question and Answer, word rhythm patterns, and the melodic setting

of songs had already taken place. The type of question
quoted above would now make use of a three chord build-up.

Group 3 Where are you going on Sa-tur-day? (sustained)
 s   s   s   s s s s   s   s

Group 2 Where are you go-ing on Sa-tur-day? (sustained)
 m   m m   m m m m m   m

Group 1 Where are you go-ing on Sa-tur-day? (sustained)
begins   d   d   d d d d   d d   d

Group 3 Where are you go-ing on Sa-tur-day? (sustained)
 d'   d' d' d' d' d' d' d' d'

Group 2 Where are you go-ing on Sa-tur-day? (sustained)
 l   l   l l l l l l l

Group 1 Where are you go-ing on Sa-tur-day? (sustained)
begins   f   f f   f f   f f f   f

Group 3 Where are you go-ing on Sa-tur-day? (sustained)
 r'   r' r' r' r' r' r' r' r'

Group 2 Where are you go-ing on Sa-tur-day? (sustained)
 t   t t t t t t t

Group 1 Where are you go-ing on Satur-day? (sustained)
begins   s   s s s s   s s s

Groups 4, 5, and 6 would build up their Answer in the
same way, although one teacher recalls, amusingly, a case
where the traditional harmonic tug, following the s-t-r'
Question, was such that the answering groups instantly,

unanimously and without prior consultation, replied by declaiming on top doh:

We're just not go-ing to tell you!
d'   d'   d' d'   d'   d' d' d'

Following on this exploratory build-up of chords using Question and Answer and name patterns, some children wanted to sing the composite chord beginning each note simultaneously. This demand almost always came from a minority of children in any Junior class, with the less adventurous spirits later following their example. In some instances there was no demand for the singing of the composite chord, it not occurring to the children that notes could be immediately combined in this way. In these cases the original suggestions would be made by the teacher, and some of the children would then experiment with the combined sounds, with the others learning from their experiences.

From the time when the general approach outlined in this book was first begun wide divergence was found between the time when children of differing or similar age groups in different schools, or within the same school or class, felt ready to experiment with the immediate simultaneous singing of notes forming a chord. This is but to say that the rate of development in this aspect of music making was as variable as development in all other classroom activities.

It was on occasions particularly affected by this variable, that flexible grouping of children could be used to the best advantage. Different groups in the same class could be concerned with different aspects of song-making, ranging from the creation of a melody to the use of harmony, ostinato, and other forms of musical embellishment. There could be individual contributions, and within and between groups a continuous cross-feeding of ideas. Furthermore, this type of flexible organization allowed too for the social and emotional involvement of the whole class, as a unit, in this creative expression.

Some of the first examples of the use of chordal singing in the making of songs consisted of chanting chords to a simple verse, often limericks or somewhat similar repeated rhythmic patterns. These simple repetitive word rhythms allowed the children to concentrate their effort on the harmonic side of the activity and to build up a confidence that would later allow the use of chords in setting more ambitious and expressive verse.

As in the previous *melodic* use of chord notes, the chords to be used and their points of change were discussed and experimented with by the children among themselves. Sometimes advice was sought from the teacher, with a final 'democratic' decision being arrived at.

The following is an example of a chordal chant setting which made use of the basic chords, d-m-s, f-l-d', s-t-r', and in which the children's experiments were successfully realized.

There was an Old Man with a beard

Group 3	s	s s	s	s	s s s
Group 2	m	m m	m	m	m m m
Group 1	d	d d	d	d	d d d

Who said, 'It is just as I feared!

Group 3   s ————————————————
Group 2   m————————————————
Group 1   d ————————————————

Two Owls and a Hen

Group 3   d'————————————————
Group 2   l ————————————————
Group 1   f

Four Larks and a Wren

Group 3   r'————————————————
Group 2   t ————————————————
Group 1   s ————————————————

Have all built their nests in my beard!'

Group 3   d'————————————————————
Group 2   d'————————————————————
Group 1   d ————————————————————

(Purists concerned with consecutive fifths are not invited to comment.)

Occasionally differences of opinion became such that a group would break up and form two separate groups, each with its own placing of chord changes.

Some classes attempting the chord formation, quoted above, found that *Group 1* was unable to make the change from the doh of the second line, to the fah of the third line. This leap of four notes, d-f, was something not previously experienced. When singing the chords melodically, as in d-m-s, f-l-d', the movement to fah was by step downwards from soh.

Joint consultation between children and teacher led to experiment with the chords in which the order of the chord notes was changed. For example, the chord d-m-s, with doh sung at the bottom note was now sung with me as the bottom note producing the order upwards of m-s-d', and then with soh as the bottom note producing s-d'-m'. Similar experimentation with f-l-d' and l-d'-f' occurred, and, because some voices found d'-f'-l' difficult, this version of the chord was sung eight notes lower as d-f-l. Similarly s-t-r' was transposed to t,-r-s and r-s-t.

By using, when difficulty was experienced, the version of a chord which offered the most comfortable vocal movement for any of the three parts being sung, all the children were soon able to make use of the three chords without difficulty. For those who had difficulty with the original setting of the particular limerick quoted above, more than one harmonic setting was now easily arrived at. Three examples are quoted below, the harmonies chosen to be read vertically in columns 1, 2, and 3.

There was an Old Man with a beard,

```
 1   2   3
(s) (s) (s)
(m) (m) (m)
(d) (d) (d)
```

```
 1   2   3    Who said, 'It is just as I feared!
(s) (d') (s)
(m) (s) (r)
(d) (m) (t,)
```

```
 1   2   3    Two Owls and a Hen
(l) (d') (s)
(f) (l) (m)
(d) (f) (d)
```

```
 1   2   3    Four Larks and a Wren
(s) (r') (l)
(r) (t) (f)
(t,) (s) (d)
```

```
 1   2   3    Have all built their nests in my beard!'
(s) (d') (s)
(m) (d') (m)
(d) (d) (d)
```

Some of the children later tried changes of harmony which were not line by line, and a more subtle appreciation of the effect of changing chords sometimes resulted. At the same time the experiments mentioned earlier in the chapter developed, where children explored combinations of three notes based on notes other than d, f, and s. Combinations not spaced in thirds, such as d-r-s, and four-note chords like d-m-s-t and d-m-s-l, were tried out. These were almost always experimented with using word patterns and sol-fa.

A few instances of close clusters of notes forming adventurous combinations of sounds also occurred, sometimes using notes of traditional scales sung to sol-fa names and sometimes using free-sliding 'glissando' vocal sounds, staccato interjections and the like, which did not use note names. These latter experiments were very infrequent and the majority of children's exploration remained harmonically very traditional. This was probably a reflection of their musical environment both in and out of school.

At times such experiments were regarded as being in the category of incidental sound effects, at others as valid in their own right alongside traditional harmonies.

A small but growing number of music educationists in the country hope that more encouragement may be given children of all ages to experiment with harmonies of both a selective and free nature. Already some schools in various parts of the country provide wide opportunities for the development of aural perception and self-expression through sound. It must nevertheless be emphasized that most children involved in the approach reported in this book were inclined towards traditional harmonies. Even those with an eager desire to experiment freely with combined sounds found themselves more capable of doing so after early experiment with the simple and easily sung traditional chords.

Having experimented with chordal changing of words, first using simple word patterns as in the limerick and then using these sounds more subtly in association with their own words, the children later used harmony in song settings with voice and instruments. Further comment on this will be made in the last chapter.

Before leaving this area of harmonic exploration, however, it would be well to look at one further experiment, made by a number of children, on the relationship between harmony and melody. This concerned improvisation on a harmonic base, which was somewhat reminiscent, in an elementary way, of certain forms of jazz.

IMPROVISATION ON A HARMONIC FRAMEWORK

A number of children would establish a harmonic progression, using words or sol-fa names, such as follows:

Part 3	s	s	s	s	s
Part 2	m	m	m	m	m
Part 1	d	d	d	d	d
	quick	slow	quick	slow	slow

Part 3	s	s	s	s	s
Part 2	m	m	m	m	m
Part 1	d	d	d	d	d
	quick	slow	quick	slow	slow

Part 3	s	s	s	s	s
Part 2	r	r	r	r	r
Part 1	t,	t,	t,	t,	t,
	quick	slow	quick	slow	slow

Part 3   s ————————————
Part 2   m ————————————
Part 1   d ————————————

sustained.

Various children would then attempt individually to improvise a melody over this repeated harmonic framework. Sol-fa names were not used for the melody and the improviser sang on any suitable syllable.

The pleasure which some children found in this type of expression and the facility with which the improvisers spontaneously created a melody related to the harmonic base, was often remarkable. The number of children who found this type of improvisation satisfying and easy would form, at the outset, some 10 per cent to 20 per cent of the class. It was interesting to note that the most successful improvisers included less academically able children, as well as some of average or high attainment. One recalls a 9-year-old boy, receiving specific remedial help with reading during part of the week, who derived great pleasure from this type of improvised vocal expression. His absorption of the sounds of the chord progressions of the harmonic base, and the resultant melodic facility with which he improvised, was quite exceptional.

This type of improvisation by Juniors was attempted only over a very simple harmonic base. No attempt was made to notate the improvised melody, as the essence of the activity at this stage was its spontaneity. Contrasts of melody, harmony, texture, and accompaniment, characteristic of more thoughtful creative expression, was not attempted by improvisers of Junior age. These did, however, occur at Secondary level.

NOTATION

Chapter 3 referred to forms of notation, and this chapter might well end by discussing further the place of notation.

First, however, it should be made quite clear that lack of familiarity with orthodox staff notation on the part of teachers or children need not be a hindrance. It is the creative expression *through sound* that is of primary importance. Some of the most exciting work observed has developed in classrooms where neither teacher nor children were familiar with staff notation although many of them learned to use it in an elementary form through experiment. But when children did learn to notate, it was found that it helped them to organize and extend the creative use of their sound experiences.

The first form of notation used with the selective approach was that of the traditional hand signs which accompanied the sung Question and Answer. This notation merely showed differences in the relative pitch of sung words. It did not show differences in rhythm although, of course, such differences were present, as sound, in the sung rhythm of the words. Next the sol-fa names associated with the signs were used, as in the Question and Answer about the 'red squirrel' quoted in Chapters 2 and 3. Here the physical symbols acquired names.

Some teachers using the selective approach did not take notation further than this point. They were satisfied with the pitch being notated through sol-fa and the rhythm implicit in the words. When using voices without words or when using instruments it then became necessary for the children to memorize the word rhythms in order to use them as abstract rhythms with or without pitch.

When using free Question and Answer some teachers and children experimented with approximate notation. An early example of this was:

Question by teacher 'What are your favourite sweets?'

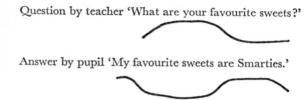

Answer by pupil 'My favourite sweets are Smarties.'

The lines under the words indicate the approximate rise and fall of the voice, this being, in the case of the pupil, a free response. It was interesting to note that, certainly at the outset, the vast majority of pupils replied by imitating the melodic line of the teacher, in spite of it being suggested that they respond freely. The confidence to respond freely usually developed after the use of a selective approach.

The free responses, which depended perhaps even more than the selective on the stimulus and confidence generated between teacher and pupil or pupil and pupil, were sometimes also notated by using sol-fa rather than approximate notation. This depended on the ability of the teacher and pupils to recognize relationships between sounds which might form a florid melodic line. Whichever form of notation was used, its employment was always a secondary process following on the creative work.

Difficulties of notation often became more acute when attempts were made to notate the rhythm in addition to the pitch. When the words involved complex rhythms some children and teachers, as already stated, were content to rely on the word patterns as a means of recalling the rhythms. Where the sung rhythms were simple enough many teachers encouraged the children to attempt to notate rhythm *and* pitch. It was often found that, as in the notation of pitch, the visual image helped children to become more consciously aware of differences of rhythm and this assisted the recall and further development of rhythmic patterns created by themselves.

The necessity or desirability of rhythmic notation, from a purely creative point of view, may be debatable. Many teachers felt that when children notated their own work this helped to relate the creative aspect of music making to the interpretive side, the singing and playing of 'composed' pieces of music. Indeed many would argue that familiarity with music notation should be associated from the start with the notating of children's own work rather than through formal sight-reading books.

Some examples of the notation by children of their own work are quoted here. Those readers who have no interest in the notation of creative work may move on to the next chapter. Pitch notation sometimes began with a two-line stave. This would mean that examples of word patterns would be notated first through illustration by the teacher and then by the children working individually or in groups:

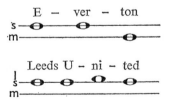

Some Infant teachers encouraged the use of different colours for notes of different pitch.

Not all teachers were happy with the idea of a stave progressing from two lines, and used the five-line stave from the outset. Other teachers wished the actual rather than relative pitch to be notated, and introduced the treble clef from the outset. Some children preferred the five-line stave, others a more limited stave.

Differences in rhythm were usually identified through the teacher asking children to discover which were the 'quicker' or 'slower' words in a jingle or song they had made up. Some teachers identified these directly as ♫ and ♩, though being very conscious that the duration of each note was dependent on the general tempo of the words. Although the use of 'quick' and 'slow' might offend purists, they felt that sophisticated explanation of the relative time duration of notes could be left for a later date and that singing the song at different speeds was all the explanation needed.

Our previous football team jingles would then be notated possibly as:

E   — ver — ton,   Leeds   U   —   ni   —   ted
quick   quick   slow   quick   quick   quick   quick

With the orthodox notation used instead of the above, this particular rhythmic form of the words would read

E-ver-ton   Leeds U – ni – ted

Quavers, if occurring in pairs, were usually joined irrespective of syllabic divisions. Note that this particular rhythmic interpretation of 'Everton, Leeds United' is only one of many ways of saying or singing the words.

The use of football team names led almost inevitably to the children's singing: 'We are the champions'. The rhythm of this sung phrase was worked out as:

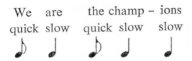

and notated with pitch as

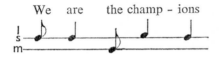

Following are the various stages of notation, illustrated through a simple verse made up by a group of Juniors and notated by them. This verse was given two different tunes created as complementary to each other and sung in 2 parts. Tune 1 is quoted here.

CHRISTMAS SONG

Christmas time is so much fun
d·   d   m m s   s   d'

Santa Claus is on his way
d' d'   s   s d d   r

Tinsel on the Christmas tree
m m s   s   m· m   s

Bells are ringing loud and clear
m   d   s s   m   m   d

Christmas time is so much fun

San - ta Claus is on his way

Tin - sel on the Christmas tree

Bells are ringing loud and clear

The tune minus the words notated on a five-line stave using the treble clef:

Christmas Song   First tune

d   d   m   m   s   s   d'   d' d' s   s   d   d   r

m   m   s   s   m   m   s   m d s   s   m   m   d

It might be worth quoting the second tune, although out of context here, to illustrate the exploration of intervals by the children as an approach to part singing.

Although very much a play on the intervals obtained from the use of d-m-s-d', the children were quite adamant about the need for the combined use of d, r, at the end of the second line, and of m, r, at the beginning of the third line. It was, however, not always clear whether this was motivated by the melodic shape, or the specific wish to sound these particular intervals.

Here is another example of how a song already quoted earlier in this chapter was notated by one of the Junior children at *actual pitch*. The girl responsible for writing out the song setting became familiar with the need to use an F sharp through playing the song on a set of chimebars. The sol-fa and rhythm are notated together and the tune minus words is then written on the stave with treble clef signature.

JABBERWOCKY

Jabberwock, Jabberwock, great big ·ug-ly beast
m   m   m   s   s   s   d   d   r   r   m

Eyes of flame and teeth like spears

Massive spikes and claws of steel

Please don't make a feast of me

Jobberwock Jobberwock great big ugly beast

Eyes of flame and teeth like spears

Massive spikes and claws of steel

please dont make a feast of me

Various uses of ostinato were sometimes notated on the same sheet of paper as the tune, as for example in another setting of the same verse, where a repetitive accompaniment using a second vocal group and an instrumental player was used. Under the notated tune was written

Apart from ostinato, different parts, or introductions or conclusions to the basic tune, were always written out on separate sheets of paper, as required by whoever was involved in that particular activity. No attempt at a composite score was ever made, the children relying on each other to make individual or group contributions.

If children used sounds in free vocal or instrumental experiment that neither they nor the teacher could notate in sol-fa or staff notation, this was not regarded as detracting from the value of the sound experiment as such. This usually occurred when the children were using sounds not related to orthodox scale patterns. Here the exact pitch of the notes or the relationship between them was unimportant—the general shape and resultant 'atmosphere' of the sounds was the predominant factor in determining children's choice. Where the sounds could not be notated in any conventional way, they were made available for recall by (*a*) memorizing the shape and quality of the sounds (*b*) making a tape recording or (*c*) improvising approximate notation as referred to earlier in free Question and Answer.

Example of approximate notation

Harmonic shape sung on 'lee' sound, in this case not acting as an accompaniment but as an interlude between two stanzas of an evocative nature.

High 'lee'

Middle 'lee'

Low 'lee'

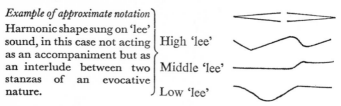

The duration of this sort of composite sound would be governed by the words, if accompanied, or, when not accompanying words as above, by a decision as to its time span, usually in seconds. It did not occur to the children, or they did not find it necessary, to indicate the number of seconds' duration on paper, as is often seen in the notation of contemporary music composed *for* children.

One of the outcomes of the use of notation was that songs, either with pitch notated in sol-fa, or with pitch *and* rhythm notated on the stave, or (rarely) with exploratory notation, were to be seen attractively displayed on classroom and corridor walls, often with colourful related art work. Some children kept individual or group song books in which the songs could be written down for reference purposes before they were replaced on the walls by new songs.

Music exists emphemerally in time. This type of notated recording that could be *seen* on wall display or in children's books was found to be valuable as a stimulus to further creative expression. Not only did this use of notation provide a store of creative experience to be recalled at will, but it made permanent the growing number of child-created songs, some of which were added to the songs, folk and composed, that were a regular part of the children's other musical activities.

5 Instruments and Voices

The experiment, on which this book is a comment, was based on the use of the voice as a medium of creative musical expression. This was done for its own sake, to explore a particularly rewarding aspect of musical creativity. It was done, too, because it was felt that the creative vocal use of sol-fa names would help to develop the children's aural perception in a way that instrumental creative work would not. Further, the teacher could easily check this aural pitch development by singing a phrase on an indeterminate vowel sound and asking the children to respond silently with the appropriate hand signs. This type of assessment took only a few seconds.

Two other factors influenced the nature of the experiment. It was not dependent on a financial outlay to cover the purchase of instruments; and the inevitable use of words implied a close relationship between the music and creative expression through language. It would, however, have been foolish to reject the use of available instruments. Contrasts of texture occur between individual voices, but instruments can add further welcome 'colour' contrast.

For the reasons already given, in particular because of the wish to associate musical creativity with the development of aural pitch discrimination, the actual *creation* of melody and harmony was made vocally. Instruments were used as ancillary means of 'orchestrating' the work already created. This chapter deals with the introduction of instruments in this sense, and also with the relation of creative music making to other means of creative expression.

The work involved in the experiment was initially largely dependent on in-service training courses for teachers. These were mainly non-residential, and consisted of four to six sessions of one and a half hours' duration each, arranged locally and taking place in a conveniently situated school. Following on the initial impetus teachers often developed their work on individual lines. These courses were not in lecture form but involved teachers in group activity in which *they themselves* created music using the vocal approach.

Instruments were used to embellish what was created vocally, and the words to be set were of adult interest and often selected by the teachers. On a limited number of residential courses successful attempts were made by teachers to set words of a more continuous nature, producing work of a choral or operatic nature.

OSTINATO

Both instruments and voices can embellish vocal word settings. The embellishments in our experiment commonly took the form of ostinato. The word 'ostinato' is here used loosely to indicate repetitive or sustained sounds which may (*a*) introduce a song, (*b*) act as a background, or (*c*) serve as a conclusion. What is said in the following pages about ostinato can also, however, be often applied to accompaniments, introductions, or conclusions which were *not* repetitive in nature and which might include a second or third melody or a harmonic accompaniment changing appropriately to the melodic changes.

Three basic types of ostinato were used, each of which could be divided into two or more varieties. The ostinato might employ (*a*) rhythm only, (*b*) pitch only, of a melodic or harmonic nature, or both, (*c*) rhythm and pitch combined, which also might be of a melodic or harmonic nature, or both, enlivened by rhythmic characteristics. These three basic types could, in their turn be (*a*) vocal (*b*) instrumental (*c*) vocal and instrumental.

The permutations possible from the combinations quoted above are such that many pages might be devoted to examples of them. What is given below is a selection of examples used, extracted from the complete compositions. This is followed by a complete example of a very simple song-setting, embellished equally simply but effectively by 9-year-old children attempting to use ostinato techniques for the first time with the song they had created vocally.

It is hoped that the simplicity of this approach will stimulate the imagination of the reader without lengthy quotations of other examples.

1. *Rhythmic ostinato*

(*a*) *Vocal*, using chanted words derived from the verse set, or rhythmic vocal sounds.
  e.g. bim—ba—ba—bom,—m—ba,—m—ba.

(*b*) *Instrumental* using non-pitch percussion instruments such as tambourines, or hand drums.
  Many instruments suitable for this sort of use were made by the children. These included 'shakers', rhythm sticks, and others, some of which had been suggested by participation in some of the BBC Music for Schools programmes.

(*c*) *Vocal and Instrumental* using various combinations of the above and allowing much room for experiment which revealed at times a not too deeply hidden primitive subconscious. With the voice, words or rhythmic vocal sounds were used. Here is a simple example:

> >		
oo—ra—ra, oo—ra—ra	x x	〰〰
voices	drum	shakers

2. *Pitch Ostinato*

(a) *Vocal.* This might use a simple lulling and repetitive s-m sound sung to words or vowel sounds. It might make use of a sustained chord with the notes sung simultaneously or built up from the lowest note. The sustained chord, in its simplest form on the notes d m s, would be sung to words or sounds such as 'lee'. If the words were appropriate, a more discordant combination of sounds might be sung possibly making use of an increase or decrease of volume or both, e.g.

sung on 'lee' or an evocative word like 'frighten'.

(b) *Instrumental.* A lulling figure similar to the vocal interval in 2 (a) above was often used, sometimes with alternation between the sound of a metal pitch percussion instrument, such as the glockenspiel or chime bars, and a wood instrument like the xylophone.

The children were encouraged to consider carefully the sound textures of the various instruments, and not to make arbitrary decisions as to combinations of sounds but to relate their choice to the 'atmosphere' of the music created.

For this type of ostinato it was found that the recorder was often ideally suitable, and children of a very early age, or complete beginners, were able to make an instrumental contribution to the music.

Harmonies could also be played instrumentally, with the same consideration being given to sound textures.

(c) *Vocal and Instrumental.* This area offered an excellent
opportunity to explore the contrasts of texture of individual instruments in various combinations. This was
easier when the attention of the children was not dis-
tracted by the rival attraction of rhythmic variation.

In the following example the doh G was given by the
xylophone, and so the l-s of the voice was E'-D'. The
length of the sustained notes for recorder and voice was
determined by experiment and related to the words of
the song

3. *Rhythm and Pitch Ostinato*

This area of exploration can be regarded as adding pitch
differences to the type of rhythmic ostinato quoted, 1 (a)–(c)
above, or of adding rhythm to the pitch ostinato of 2 (a)–(c)
above.

(a) *Vocal rhythm and pitch.* The example quoted uses sung and
spoken words and vocal 'sounds'.

Words sung to the sol-fa sounds noted	Through the forest, through the forest l s m m, l s m m,
Words spoken	slith-'ring————, slith-'ring————,
Voices 1 and 2 in turn singing the written sounds to the sol-fa notes given	(1) bim-ba-ba-bom (2) m-ba, m-ba, d d d r m r, m r,

(*b*) *Instrumental rhythm and pitch.* Both non-pitch and pitch instruments were available. The rhythm was often, but not always, derived from words occurring in the verse set vocally. In the example given the rhythm was derived from the words, 'Are you afraid?' 'No, No—No No!'

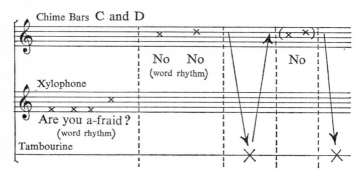

The above type of ostinato was rarely notated although some individual children would make their own notation of the notes used for particular word rhythms. Normally the children would rely on each other and continual experiment in deciding *when* their particular contribution was required.

(*c*) *Vocal and Instrumental rhythms and pitch.* As in instrumental rhythms and pitch, no notated score was prepared although some children found it useful to make a note of their own individual or group contribution. Here is a rough transcript of a typical example:

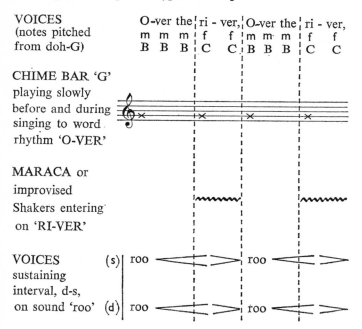

VOICES (notes pitched from doh-G)

O-ver the ri - ver, O-ver the ri - ver,
m m m f f m m m f f
B B B C C B B B C C

CHIME BAR 'G' playing slowly before and during singing to word rhythm 'O-VER'

MARACA or improvised Shakers entering on 'RI-VER'

VOICES sustaining interval, d-s, on sound 'roo'

(s) roo   roo
(d) roo   roo

Written down in this way the above example may perhaps look a little complicated to those not familiar with this type of scoring. In practice, however, it is anything but complicated, although it takes some time in experiment and rejection until a final decision is reached. But this time is well spent, both in developing the children's sensibility of musical expression and in the insight it gives them, in microcosm, into the problems facing composers.

Having decided on the pitch for setting the words 'over the river', ending on the inconclusive fah, the slow sound G—G was used to repeatedly introduce and accompany the phrase. To give an eerie quality to the word 'river' a sustained shake was added as that word was sung. As a way of heightening the mysterious atmosphere other voices singing the word 'roo' on the combined notes 'doh' and 'soh' accompanied the singing of the words. It was found that increasing and decreasing the volume of the 'roo' interval of d-s, would produce an even more disturbed atmosphere especially as sounded against the 'fah' on which 'river' was sung.

The examples quoted give a cross-section of the possibilities inherent in this type of creative work. They are capable of many more variations and developments. But to illustrate the *starting point* for this type of embellishment of songs created vocally the following example is quoted in its entirety.

This was the first attempt by 9-year-olds at embellishing a simple song. The children concerned had become familiar with the melodic singing of patterns derived from d r m s l but no harmonic singing had yet been attempted. The words are not the children's but are taken from a verse by Michael Flanders which interested them. The words were spaced as follows:

> Lon-don Tran-sport
> s   l   s   m
>
> Die-sel en-gined
> s   l s   m
>
> Nine-ty se-ven horse-power
> d   d d   d   m   s
>
> Om-ni-bus
> l l   s
>
> Hold ve-ry tight please
> d   d d   s   s
>
> Ting ting ting.
> m   r   d

The last phrase of the song, 'ting, ting, ting' to m-r-d, was tried out as an accompaniment to the sung words, first as a vocal accompaniment, and then as an instrumental accompaniment using only tabors to the rhythm of the words. The rhythm of 'hold very tight please' was played on a long open-ended drum. Chime bars experimented with the rhythm and pitch of the first phrase of the song, 'London Transport', and glockenspiels with the rhythm and pitch of 'ting, ting, ting'. Maracas, claves, and various drums explored the rhythmic possibilities of the words of the verse, with the almost inevitable recourse to a cymbal clash for the end of the whole piece.

What finally emerged was a combination of sung words, spoken words, pitch and non-pitch percussion. Being an early attempt it was much simpler than some of the examples quoted in the section on 'Ostinato'. There was no experiment with combined sung vocal sounds, and instruments, with one exception, were used separately. Nevertheless the basic elements of contrasting modes of expression are all present.

The events quoted below were not always adhered to in the order given.

Long open-ended Drum	rhythm of 'Hold very tight please'
Tabors	rhythm of 'ting, ting, ting'
Chimebars	Lon-don Tran-sport

	s	l	s	m
	G	A	G	E

| Xylophone | repeats phrase of chimebars |
| Glockenspiels | 'ting, ting, ting' (repeated) |

	m	r	d
	E	D	C

All sing the whole of the song unaccompanied.

⎰ Maracas ⎱   ⎰ rhythm of 'ting, ting, ting'   ⎱
⎱ Claves ⎰   ⎱ rhythm of 'Hold very tight please' ⎰

Large group speaks words of the song accompanied by a small group singing 'ting, ting, ting', to m r d

Small bongos	rhythm of 'Hold very tight please'
Kettledrum	rhythm of 'London Transport' (repeated)
Cymbal	X!

INTEGRATION AND CONTINUITY

A look now at the ways in which the creative setting of songs was used in a more continuous context, involving various aspects of story, movement, handcraft and drama.

In the Infant examples quoted, instruments were not used because they were not available. In one or two instances at Junior level where instruments *were* available, it was felt that the first attempts, of any length, at combining music with activities in other media should not be made more complicated by introducing instruments too early. It was realized that such work could later be enhanced through the use of varying instrumental and vocal combinations.

'RED INDIAN SAGA' (5–6-YEAR-OLDS)

The Red Indian Saga developed with a class of 5–6-year-olds at a very early stage when the selective vocabulary was based on no more than the singing of Question and Answer to s-m with the appropriate hand signs. The Saga was sparked off by one of the children suddenly saying to the teacher: 'Miss. You look like a Red Indian making those signs!' During the next 'Movement session' the children moved to the sung sounds of s-s-m-m and variations on them, produced with great fun and accompanied by non-pitch percussion. Hand signs were in use and one of the boys sang:

'I am In-dian brave'
s m s   s   m

to the sounds given. This rhythm pattern was taken up by the other children and further 'Red Indian' phrases were added:

'I am In-dian squaw'
s m s   s   m

sang one of the girls and eventually a third line of similar rhythm emerged with some variation of pitch:

We are In-dian braves
s   m   s   s   m

We are In-dian squaws
s   m   s   s   m

We build to-tem pole
s   s   s s   m

The song was later written down on the chalk board after, as the teacher said, 'All the activity and experience of feeling it and singing it.'

The movement and music became extended in a characterized narrative form. After the activity of the day, night came and the Indian village settled down to sleep. From the movement came the feeling of sinking down which in the most natural way suggested to the children the sounds of a descending, 'Go to sleep', sung as m-r-d. The children were not aware of the names of the sounds used, so the teacher gave them these names and showed them the hand signs to help them remember this sound pattern.

To 'Go to sleep' were added words forming the same rhythm and pitch pattern as, 'We are Indian braves' producing

Mo-ther wat-ches you
s   m   s   s   m

Different groups of children combined these producing their first acquaintance with 'part-singing'.

$$
\left\{
\begin{array}{l}
\text{Mo-ther wat-ches you,} \\
\text{s\quad m\quad s\quad s\quad m} \\
\text{Go to\quad sleep ———,} \\
\text{m\quad r\quad\quad d ———,}
\end{array}
\right\}
$$

Into the village crept a brown bear

Brown bear won't hurt you
s   m   s   s   m

He wants com-pa-ny
s   m   s   s   m

To continue in the words of the teacher:

'And so it grew. We collected books, pictures of tepees. It was Summer term and out of doors we joined two white sheets together and printed a design on it with wooden blocks, adding painted animals.

'Everyone brought an old white shirt from home, fringed it, printed it. Long twigs were collected to make bows. It was discovered that some kinds of wood bent and some snapped.

'Feathers were collected from the fields to make head-dresses. There were plenty of magpies about and we even got some gorgeous pheasant feathers and, from various sources, guinea fowl, peacock feathers and so on.

'Using the making of head-dresses, various musical ways of counting up to ten were devised and the project occupied us for a whole term. It covered Music, Movement (I hate traditional Music and Movement), Geography, creative work with their hands, Number, and other related fields.

'By the end of the term the notes lah and top doh were in use, making the children's selective vocabulary d-r-m-s-l-d', sung with hand signs and using the five-line stave from the word go.

'There was no one in the class with any inhibitions about singing out loud—they all pitched almost perfectly. It was a most happy term. Then they had to move up.'

'SARAH AND THE WITCH' (6-YEAR-OLDS)

The story of 'Sarah and the Witch' was referred to in Chapter 4. It was written by one 6-year-old girl. When it had been read out the teacher suggested to the rest of the children that it might be made into a musical story. As time went on the story was elaborated in various ways by the children.

The class involved had been working with the creative approach reported in this book for some twelve months. The approach generally had been selective with occasional use of the free approach. Acquaintance with d r m f s l t d' had been established and the children were accustomed to experimenting with interesting word rhythms and setting them to music.

Following on the initial written framework of the story, the work, apart from the notating of songs with sol-fa, was oral. What follows is an attempt at producing an adult written transcript of the children's musical story as it finally emerged with all its sublime illogicalities. Included is as much of the original phraseology as can be recalled, but one can only apologize for the occasional flatness of the transcript by comparison with the oral vivacity of the original. The songs are exactly as composed and notated.

Sarah was a little girl who lived near a forest. She had a dog who played with her in the forest and they had great times together. Quite near to this forest lived a wicked witch who used to disguise herself as a poor old woman and then get people to follow her to her palace.

When she got them there she turned them into stone until she needed them to work for her. Then she turned them back into people for just as long as she required them to work for her.

The trees of the forest knew all about the wicked witch and on this day she was searching for a fresh victim.

The trees loved Sarah and they didn't want the witch to catch her and in sweet soft voices they sang to her

> Take care Sa-rah
> s   m   s   m

and the grasses replied sadly

> Sa-rah wouldn't lis-ten
> m m   r   r   d d

(These two phrases were also sung together in parts.)

The witch came disguised as a poor old woman of course, and sang to Sa-rah

          Would you like to come to my pa-lace?
          s   s   s s   l   l   l   s   m

and Sarah answers

          Yes I would
          m r   d

          Thank you ve-ry much
          m   m   r r   d

Then Sarah asks

          May I take my pet dog Susie?
          s   s   s   s   l l   s m

to which the Witch replies

                Yes you may
                m   r   d

and Sarah, because she was polite, sang again

          Thank you ve-ry much
          m   m   r r d

The Witch takes Sarah to the Palace and gives her some magic cake which puts her partly into the witch's power. But as she is sitting there a little bird with a broken wing sings to her through the window.

He sings

          Go to the *white scream-ing moun-tain* [*sic*]
          s s s   l   l   l   s   m

          There you will see an old man
          m   m   m f f   f   m

          He has the cure to get you out of here
          r   r   r   m r d d m m s

          So go Sa-rah go
          s d′ s   m d

Sarah realized that she was in danger and so she decided that she must escape and find the old man of the white screaming mountain.

She followed the little bird until she came to the foot of the mountain. It was here where the bird said he could go on no longer and Sarah must travel up the mountain alone.

As she reached the top she saw an old man sitting there and so she sang to him

> A little bird told me
> s s s   l   l   s
>
> That you'd be sure to help
>   m   s   s l   l s

to which he replied

> What do you want
>   d d   d   d
>
> What do you want
>   d d   d   d
>
> What do you want from me?
>   d   d   d   d   d d

Meanwhile the little bird had returned to the path and there he met a charming prince who was always on the look-out for damsels in distress.

The little bird sang to him

> Sa-rah is under a spell
> s   s   s   l l l   s
>
> Go to the white screa-ming moun-tain
> s s s   l   l   l   s   m
>
> There you will see a ve-ry old man
>   d   r   m f s l l   t   d'
>
> Sit-ting a-lone by a foun-tain
> s   s   s   s   md r   d

The Prince arrived at the fountain just as Sarah was asking for help. He could see that she was a bit afraid of the old man and so he stepped towards the old man and pleaded for his magic potion.

The old man could see that the prince was a good man and so he gave him the potion.

With only one dose of the potion Sarah was freed from the Witch's spell.

When she told the old man what had happened to her he gave her another potion. This of course was to turn the Witch into stone.

Sarah and the prince thanked the old man and returned to the Palace where they freed everyone with Magic potion number 1 and turned the Witch into stone with Magic potion number 2.

Of course Sarah and the Prince fell in love and lived happily ever after with little dog Susie.

The make-up of the story incorporated movement and some considerable art work.

The children who made up 'Sarah and the Witch' and the 'London Transport' song, and those who created the puppet music drama 'Pinocchio' which follows, were filmed at work for the BBC television series 'Music in Schools'. This series produced by John Hosier, was screened in the spring of 1969 and reshown some twelve months later.

'PINOCCHIO' (9-YEAR-OLDS)

The Pinocchio story had interested a class of 9-year-olds to the point of wanting to create from it a puppet music drama. Days were spent on making hand puppets, of considerable artistry, representing the characters in the story. The dialogue was made up orally, with the role of narrator sometimes taken by an individual, sometimes by the chorus.

At moments in the drama where it was felt that music could bring a further dimension to the spoken word, the children as a class, or in large or small groups, set the words to music, vocally. The class had been working creatively with vocal sound for some previous months both on a selective and free basis.

A Punch and Judy booth was made and, although this was not the main purpose of the various activities, performances were given for the rest of the school. Some children manipulated the skilfully made puppets, others spoke the dialogue 'backstage', and all, as characters in the drama or as a commenting chorus, sang the songs the children had created.

For reference purposes the spoken dialogue was written out as a libretto and the songs, made through a combination of a free and selective approach, were notated as charts. The help of the teacher was required for the notation of the 'free songs', *and the sol-fa names, not previously known, of notes in the song were learned and their retention made certain through use in other rhythmic phrases and through Question and Answer.*

In this puppet music drama some use was made of both pitch and non-pitch percussion.

The story is too familiar to warrant quoting the entire operetta, but below are excerpts from some of the unadorned songs.

Opening Chorus

s   l   s   f m   s
We will tell the story

m f   s s   f   m f
Of a lit-tle wood-en toy

f   f   s   f   m f   f
And of his strange ad-ven-tures

f   f   s   s   m   r   d
Un-til he be-came a boy

s   s   l s f m   s
His name it is Pin-o-chio

m   s   s   f m f
Ge-pet-to's on-ly son

f   f   s f m   f   f
And here be-fore he made him

f   f   f   s   m   r   d
Is Ge-pet-to look-ing glum!

A lyrical aria for Gepetto follows

lt d′ t   l   t m
I am get-ting old-er

m   d′ l   l   s   l
And long to have a son

m   l̂t d′ t   l   m′ t
To make my last days hap-py

      d′   l   l   s   l
Filled with lots of fun

l͡t d′   t   l   t   m
If I had a real son

  m d′   l   l   s   l
He'd fill my days with joy

  m l͡t d′   t l m′ m′ t
But if I had a wood-en one

  d′   d′   l   l   s   l
I'd treat him like a boy

l͡t   d′   t   l l   t m
My old friend Mis-ter Cherry

  m d′ l   l   s   l
Will lend a piece of wood

  m l t   d′ t͡l m′   t
And I with care will shape him

  d′d′ l   l   s l
Until he's ver-y good

It was decided to end the song by repeating the first verse. As a last illustration, here is the song of the Cricket.

  s͵ d d d   d   t͵   r
I am a wise old Crick-et

  d d   d   d t͵   r
Lis-ten to me click-it

   s   d   s   d
Click, click, click, click

  d   s   f   m   r   m d
A click, click, click, click, click-it

    (spoken: 'oops, crick-et')

  s͵   d   d   d   d t͵   r
A hun-dred years I've lived here

```
    s,    d  d  d        t,  r
This house to me ........ is dear

    s     d     s     d
Dear, dear, dear, dear

    d   s    f    m   r   m   d
And now *you-ve* come to live here.


    s,   dd  d   d t, r
Gep-ett-o will reg-ret it

    s,   d  d dd      t, r
You hor-rid lit-tle pup-pet

    s   d   s    d
Pup, pup, pup, pup

    s   f    m   r    m  d
Pup-pet won't you hop-pit


            *Pinocchio:*
    s,   d   d  dd  t,r
Get out you sil-ly flea

    s,    d   d    d   d    t,r
This house be-longs to me

    s    d    s    d
Me, me, me, me

    s    s    f   m   r   md
Take that you stu-pid flea!
```

It is difficult to convey how much fun the children had, and how interested they were in the various activities that led to the realization of this puppet 'Pinocchio'.

From a purely musical point of view it was also remarkable to see the tremendous advance in sheer musicality and aural sensitivity that was achieved, not through a pedantic formality but through such exciting creativity.

THE TYPHOON (10–11-YEAR-OLDS)

The musical story 'The Typhoon' was the work of a 'dinner break club' of 10–11-year-olds. The teacher involved with the members of the Club was not their class teacher, and the children had not during the official school time been introduced to the type of work outlined in this book. During the lunch-time meetings the approach used was predominantly the free vocal approach with the teacher helping to identify the sounds used and to notate them using sol-fa and the stave. The words and music were made up by the children 'as we went along'. In the words of the teacher concerned, it included some 'fairly violent movement, which, as all the work occurred in the break between morning and afternoon school, was essential!'

Here is a shortened version of the early part of the story in the words of the children, with a transcription of some of the songs composed.

Not so very long ago in a Country that we know of, there lived a beautiful Princess whose name was Ying San. She was small, dark, and so happy that she almost always felt as if she wanted to sing. In fact, she sang so much that her closest friends used to call her 'Me Me Ray'.

Ying San's father was the Emperor of that country and so naturally her mother was the Empress. It was a happy place and the people loved the Princess and her father and mother.

THE PRINCESS

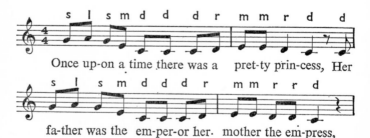

She was ver-y small, She was ver-y gay,

Ver-y ver-y dark, Me me me me ray.

Once up-on a time there was a pret-ty prin-cess.

Then one day, something dreadful happened. There was a typhoon which blew so strong and so fierce that it completely destroyed the homes of the people and left only the Royal Palace standing.

THE TYPHOON

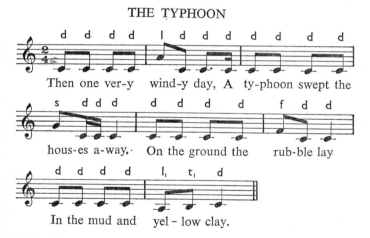

Then one ver-y wind-y day, A ty-phoon swept the

hous-es a-way. On the ground the rub-ble lay

In the mud and yel-low clay.

The Emperor who was a very gentle man grieved for his subjects when he saw their dilemma. 'What can we do—what can we do?' he said to his wife.

'Well, first of all we shall offer shelter in the Palace to the old people and the mothers with babies,' said the Empress.

'My dear, I knew that you would think of something,' said the Emperor.

'But,' said Ying San, 'that is not enough. Somehow we must rebuild the houses, though goodness knows where we shall start—there's so little of anything left.'

'Come, come,' said the Empress, 'this is not like you Ying San. We have our people, our loving talented people.'

'Yes, Mother, our talented people, and those words have provided me with inspiration. I shall go on a journey and take with me all the people who are willing and able to leave our country for a while. We shall sail to other lands and sell our skills as musicians and entertainers.'

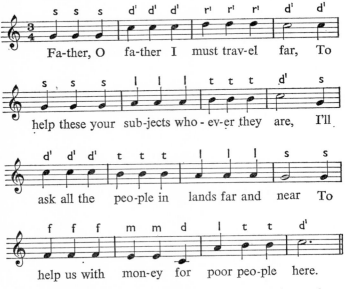

Fa-ther, O fa-ther I must trav-el far, To help these your sub-jects who-ev-er they are, I'll ask all the peo-ple in lands far and near To help us with mon-ey for poor peo-ple here.

Ying San asked her parents permission to leave and went down to the seashore where many people were gathered together. When they saw her coming they called to her, 'Come, Princess, and let us hear a cheerful song.'

They were so pleased to see her that she immediately felt her troubles were halved. But she told them that she wouldn't sing just then, for she had an idea which she wanted to discuss with them.

They all sat around and she put forward the suggestion that the most talented artistes should accompany her on a tour of foreign lands. They were delighted with the idea and couldn't imagine why they hadn't thought of it themselves. There and then they all agreed that an audition should be held in the Palace the following morning.

The day dawned bright and fair and it seemed almost like a Feast Day as the crowds moved towards the Palace gates.

The first person to be auditioned was a Strong Man. He sang to his audience in a deep bass voice.

THE STRONG MAN

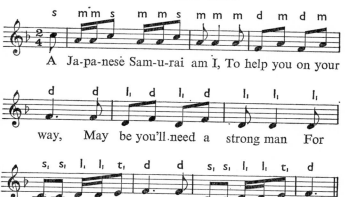

A Ja-pa-nese Sam-u-rai am I, To help you on your way, May be you'll need a strong man For I a drag-on can slay, Yes I a drag-on can slay.

To summarize the remainder of the story: in addition to the Strong Man, the people auditioned and accepted were a Fire Eater who sang his song 'in a kind of hot plum pie voice', a fabulous new Pop Group made up of Sing Hi, Sing Lo, and Sing So, and a Clown. 'The Clown twisted and tumbled his way to the throne. He fell over his big brown boots, he got his arms mixed up in his saffron gown and his cap simply would not stay on his head for more than a few seconds at a time.'

THE FIRE EATER

s   d' s m d   s s   s d'   s m   d

I am a fire— eat-er,· I swal-low tongues of

l   s   d' s m d   l l   l l

flame,   They dis - ap-pear in - side me   And I

s   f   m   r   d

blow them out a - gain.

THE CLOWN

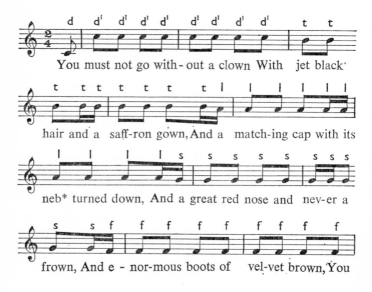

d d' d' d' d'   d' d' d' d'   t t

You must not go with- out a clown With   jet black·

t t t t   t t   t l   l l   l l l

hair and a saff-ron gown, And a   match-ing cap with its

l l   l l   s s   s s   s s s

neb* turned down, And a great red nose and nev-er a

s   s f   f f   f f   f f f   f

frown, And e - nor-mous boots of   vel-vet brown, You

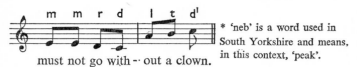

must not go with -· out a clown.

* 'neb' is a word used in South Yorkshire and means, in this context, 'peak'.

Unfortunately no transcript of the song of the Pop Group is available for illustration.

The party eventually set off, 'in the Emperor's fastest boat manned by a most skilful crew'. Everyone practised during the sea journey until in a great storm they were all shipwrecked on an island ruled by a genial wizard.

THE GENIAL WIZARD

I am a ge-nial wiz-ard, I'll help in a-ny way I can, I live on this is-land of par-a-dise But I'm not a lone-ly man, I clap my hands for danc-ers, I stamp my feet for food, I nod my head for wa-ter, And I'm nev-er in a nas-ty mood.

The genial wizard set them various tasks. The Fire Eater ate his way through a barrier of fire. Sing Hi, Sing Lo, Sing So, sang so well that they shattered a glass barrier and so on.

All were rewarded by the wizard with diamonds and gold and they returned home triumphantly.

These examples are an attempt to illustrate as simply as possible some of the ways in which children and teachers allied their musical creativity with other media to express themselves in a more continuous and integrated context. It can be seen that it was not necessary to wait for the children to acquire expertise before attempting this kind of work. The example of 'The Indian Saga' is enough indication of this. As further exploration into harmonies and various forms of accompaniments develops, more elaborate works are made possible, but the essence of the marriage of media, polygamous at times, is to be seen in the four examples given.

Conclusion

The approach described in this book is open to teachers with widely different degrees of acquaintance with music, whether it be an untutored interest or a specialist dedication. No pedagogic method is spelled out to invite unimaginative adherence.

What *is* recorded is a framework within which individual teachers can invite experiment from their children and within which they themselves can experiment and learn. The essential requirement is an imaginative and creative mind and a desire to stimulate children to express themselves through sound, language and other media.

Musical expression founded on vocal creativity will develop aural perception which will itself feed back and make available to children a greater sensitivity of expression through sound.

The degree to which the work created can be notated for future reference depends on the advice which can be offered by the teacher. This advice may be expert or it may be restricted to pitch notation through sol-fa only. Irrespective of the degree of expertise in the sphere of notation, this approach was seen to encourage integration with other activities and the eagerness with which the children took to this form of creative expression added a new dimension to their music-making.

Perhaps one of the truest educational yardsticks is the impact that an activity in school has on the developing personality of an individual child and his adjustment to the social environment. The outward manifestation of this was to be seen first in the children's increasing desire to express themselves musically, and secondly, in the vivacity of response to the challenge presented by the demands of creative musical expression. That this challenge and its problems were solved in an atmosphere of fun and excitement, in which many children contributed to a solution that often required social as well as artistic adjustment, is enough to encourage the hope that other teachers and children will venture to experiment in ways similar to those recorded in this book.

Under the aegis of the Faculty of Education at the University College of North Wales, Bangor, a curriculum development project following this approach and entitled 'Music and Creativity with children of 5–13 years old' was set up in September 1969. This project has produced, in some 80 schools of the North Wales counties, further exciting creative work bringing together music and related activities. It extended over two terms, but at its successful termination consultation between Music Organizers and Teachers' Groups in the counties led to proposals to extend the work further on a Local Authority basis. The outcome of these developments is awaited expectantly.

TABLE OF HAND SIGNS

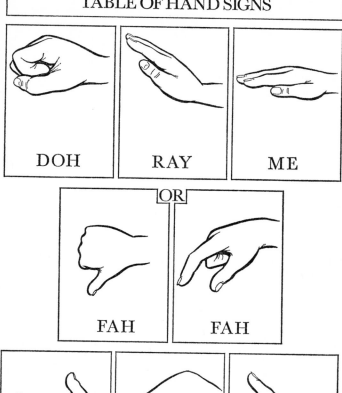

DOH   RAY   ME

OR

FAH   FAH

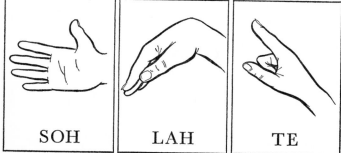

SOH   LAH   TE